Skaug's new volum
Big Ten: Critical Qu
of the most difficult issues people will have to confront. This
topic has become very popular and controversial in recent
years, but Skaug has written a very clear and convincing
argument for the certainty of Hell in general and more
specifically answers the question *How Could a Loving God
Send Anyone to Hell?* The first four chapters lay the biblical
groundwork for Skaug's ultimate answer—not only can He,
but God's character actually demands that sin be punished.

Right in the heart of the book (Chapter 5) Skaug
provides the practical and pastoral answer of how to escape
the eternal punishment of Hell. Then the following chapters
deal with the eternality of Hell and Universalism, both
important and extremely controversial questions in modern
society. Possibly the best part of the book is the Appendix at
the back that answers seven of the most pertinent questions
on the topic.

This book provides thoroughly biblical answers to this
extremely relevant issue and would be excellent resource for
those trying to work through this topic or have friends that
are struggling with it.

Paul D. Wegner
Distinguished Professor of Old Testament, Gateway Seminary of
the Southern Baptist Convention

Hell is often misunderstood or rejected outright today. Ben
Skaug helps us see that the doctrine of hell fits with what the
Bible teaches about who God is, with the teaching of Jesus,

and with the nature of human beings. Indeed, the message of the gospel doesn't make sense without the doctrine of hell. Here is a book on hell that needs to be read, digested, believed, and acted upon.

Thomas R. Schreiner
James Buchanan Harrison Professor of New Testament Interpretation
Associate Dean, The Southern Baptist Theological Seminary,
Louisville, Kentucky

The historic Christian doctrine of hell raises eyebrows, scorn, and sometimes tempers. It is usually avoided or marginalized, since it might feel too embarrassing to believe in hell in such a tolerant society. For downright honest people, though, hell raises questions. The most common is the topic and title of this book: *How Could a Loving God Send Anyone to Hell?* Thankfully, Dr. Ben Skaug authentically and patiently wrestles with this question. With fitting angst and biblical insight, he also addresses related questions and unpacks the questions behind the question: Is there really a hell? Is it biblical? Is it consistent with the biblical portrait of a loving God? Did Jesus actually teach it? Did the apostles teach it? Has the church consistently believed it? Is it really forever? Who goes there? The treatment is perceptive yet clear, straightforward yet gentle, and biblical yet fresh. Those genuinely seeking answers will find help here.

Christopher W. Morgan
Dean and Professor of Theology, California Baptist University,
Riverside, California
author and/or editor of more than twenty books including *Hell Under Fire* and *Is Hell for Real?*

With a pastor's heart and theologian's precision, Ben Skaug takes on challenging questions about life after death in this insightful book. His answers are biblical, forthright, and sobering. As you read, expect to be challenged intellectually. More importantly, prepare to be moved emotionally by the plight of unbelievers who have yet to receive the gospel. This book is a more than a theoretical treatise; it's a call to action.

Jeff Iorg
President, Gateway Seminary, Ontario, California

You can tell a lot about a church based upon what is preached from the pulpit—and what isn't. Thus, to survey the landscape of contemporary evangelicalism, it would be easy to conclude that few, if any, churches believe in a literal hell. Of course, the Scriptures as a whole, and our Lord Jesus Christ in particular, present an altogether different picture. Thankfully, Ben Skaug presents a compelling and biblical case for a literal hell and how it is rooted in the character of God. As believers in Christ, we don't fear an eternity in hell, but the reality of it should motivate us to greater evangelistic witness. *How Could a Loving God Send Anyone to Hell?* provides just such motivation for the reader.

Jason Allen
President, Midwestern Baptist Theological Seminary, Kansas City, Missouri

To grasp God's ways requires God's wisdom. On the troubling subject of hell, this book lays out the Bible's clear statements, teachings, warnings, and encouragements. The presentation is clear, logical, and thorough. Read this book to gain fresh understanding of why Jesus Christ spoke so much about hell, how his disciples applied his teachings, and what Christians today should affirm and proclaim. The gospel promise replaces unending horrors with eternal hope and joy for all who are willing to receive it.

Robert W. Yarbrough
Professor of New Testament, Covenant Theological Seminary,
St. Louis, Missouri

This book helps the Christian and the non-Christian. For the Christian, this book is a safe guide for understanding the biblical doctrine of Hell. It will encourage Christians to greater efforts in witnessing to the lost. For the non-Christian, this book is a safe guide to avoid the eternal place of punishment through Jesus, the Son of God, who died for our sins to deliver us from the wrath to come. This book accurately explains the Gospel or good news of Christ's death and resurrection for the lost sinner. This book also covers issues associated with the biblical doctrine of Hell including divine justice, the love of God, the character of God, the holiness of God, God's hatred of sin, the person of Christ, and many others. Finally, the book warns readers against false teachings about Hell, that it is a place where sinners are annihilated, or that God will save universally. In our time of spiritual decline and ruin, this book is needed and helpful.

Russell T. Fuller
Professor of Old Testament, The Southern Baptist Theological
Seminary, Louisville, Kentucky

THE BIG TEN
Critical Questions Answered

SERIES EDITORS
James N. Anderson and Greg Welty

How Could a Loving God Send Anyone to Hell?

Benjamin M. Skaug

CHRISTIAN
FOCUS

Copyright © Benjamin M. Skaug 2019

paperback ISBN 978-1-5271-0473-0
epub ISBN 978-1-5271-0508-9
mobi ISBN 978-1-5271-0509-6

Published in 2019
by
Christian Focus Publications Ltd,
Geanies House, Fearn, Ross-shire
IV20 1TW, Scotland
www.christianfocus.com

Cover design by Paul Lewis

Printed and bound by
Bell & Bain, Glasgow

CONTENTS

To Jodie and Jessica
For loving me and modeling the Christian life.
I love you both more than words can express.

Acknowledgements

I want to thank the following for their help:

- The team at Christian Focus for publishing this important series.

- Series editors James N. Anderson and Greg Welty for inviting me to write this volume and for their careful editorial work throughout this project.

- Christopher Morgan for being my mentor, PhD supervisor, confidant, and dear friend.

- Immanuel Baptist Church for allowing me time to research, write, and preach through much of the content in this book.

- Julie Tilman for reading through the manuscript several times and offering helpful suggestions.

- Gateway Seminary PhD faculty for allowing me to step away momentarily from my dissertation writing to complete this project.

Introduction

The subject of hell is not one we enjoy thinking about or discussing. We do not want our loved ones (or ourselves, for that matter) to end up in hell, and perhaps it is easier on our consciences if we look for ways to dismiss the topic altogether. If we speak about hell in ways that make it seem inconceivable or intolerable, we might be able to live as though it does not exist.

While this might be true for some, I do not think it is true of you. At this moment, you are looking at this book for reasons about which I can only speculate. Perhaps someone in your life has recently passed away and you are pondering issues of the afterlife. It might be that someone you love has recently been diagnosed with cancer and you are concerned with his or her eternal destiny. Or it might be that you are quite skeptical of this thing called hell and the God who sends people there. For whatever reason, if you have ever found yourself asking the question 'How could a loving God send anyone to hell?', then this book is for you.

I do not pretend to have all of the answers, and some of the answers I give might not persuade you. But I will be honest as I give you my best understanding of how the Bible tackles the issues involved in this question.

As we look to answer why a loving God might send anyone to hell, we should know that the question itself forces us to deal with more issues than just hell. The question contains at least three parts, and our answer must likewise consist of three parts. When we start by asking, 'How could a loving God send anyone...?', we are actually dealing with a question that starts with who God is and how He loves people (hence, How could a *loving God* send *anyone* to hell?). Therefore, the first two chapters of this book will deal with the subjects of God and how we relate to Him.

The last portion of our question deals with the subject of hell (How could a loving God send anyone *to hell?*), and thus the remainder of the book will likewise focus on various aspects of hell. Chapters 3–4 will look at what the loving Jesus and the loving apostles (the disciples Jesus entrusted to proclaim His teachings) thought about hell and who might end up there. Chapter 5 will lay out how the Bible claims guilty people can escape hell. Chapters 6–7 will look, briefly, at two perspectives that attempt to change how we think about hell (annihilationism and universalism). Chapter 8 will conclude our journey by drawing together the truths from the previous seven chapters. Finally, I have also included a Frequently Asked Questions section at the conclusion of the book so that readers can find quick answers to a few of the questions they might be asking about hell.

1

Who Can Judge the World?

The famous British philosopher Bertrand Russell stated that hell creates a moral problem of viciousness for God, and that its existence speaks to God's malice:

> I really do not think that a person with a proper degree of kindliness in his nature would have put fears and terrors of that sort into the world.... I must say that I think all this doctrine, that hell-fire is a punishment for sin, is a doctrine of cruelty. It is a doctrine that put cruelty into the world and gave the world generations of cruel torture.[1]

Basically, Russell is saying that if there is a hell that includes people being punished for their sins against God, then this

---

1   Bertrand Russell, 'Why I am not a Christian', lecture given at Battersea Town Hall, London, to the National Secular Society, March 6, 1927.

says something about God's nature and character. As he sees it, the very existence of hell implies that God is malicious.

Is Russell right? Is the very existence of hell the cause of cruelty and wickedness in this world? Furthermore, does the mere existence of hell necessitate not only that God is a non-loving God but that He might be vicious as well? In short, what does the existence of hell say about God?

Certainly, Russell is not alone in this line of thinking. A simple Google search on 'top questions about hell' reveals: 'If God is truly a loving God, then why is there a hell?'; 'Can God be called "good" if He sends people to hell?'; 'If God is a loving Father, how could He send His creation to hell?'; 'Why, if God is good, does He punish people for eternity when their "crimes" against Him are finite?'

WHAT DOES THE EXISTENCE OF HELL SAY ABOUT GOD?

What does the existence of hell say about God? Before we answer this question, we must think about evil and what evil people have done to others.

The name Saloth Sar does not strike terror in the hearts of many people. His assumed names, however— 'Pol Pot' and 'Brother number one'—might cause some to remember his wicked deeds. Pol Pot was the leader of the Communistic group known as the Khmer Rouge. By 1975, Pol Pot and the Khmer Rouge had taken over much of Cambodia and its capital, Phnom Penh. By 1979, an estimated 1.5 to

3 million people had died at the hands of this evil group. Most of the bodies of those killed during this time were dumped into mass graves called 'the killing fields'.

The Khmer Rouge used Phnom Penh to house some of the concentration camps at which they conducted egregious and unimaginable crimes. S-21 was one of those concentration camps. It is estimated that twenty thousand people were rounded up and brought to S-21. Only seven survived.

The survivors of S-21 told horrific stories of the brutality of the Khmer Rouge. One of those survivors, Chum Mey, recounted in his book, *Survivor*, that the prisoners were beaten on a daily basis. The soldiers would tie the prisoners onto a metal bedspring so that they could beat, electrocute, and whip the prisoners as a means of interrogation. If the prisoners cried out in pain, they were beaten more severely. They were also bound with their hands behind their backs and stretched on 'gallows'. While hanging 15 to 20 feet high, the prisoners were left until they passed out. Then they were lowered back to the ground, where their heads were submerged into a collection of human waste until they regained consciousness. Once the prisoners regained consciousness, the process started again.

On a recent trip to Cambodia, I visited S-21 and walked through this haunting place. Each room housed a different exhibit of the atrocities committed there. Photos of actual interrogations showed the merciless torture these human beings faced. These photos, along with dried blood and leg chains that constantly bound the prisoners, are placed in the rooms so that each visitor might gain a sense of the horrendous evil that ruled the place for several years. Every room I toured added and compounded horror upon horror to the point that I had tears in my eyes and a sense of deep depression. I continued to ask myself the same question: 'How could anyone do this to another human being?'

At first, I was numb by what I saw and felt. But then my emotions (and those of the entire group) took a turn from numbness to anger. I was angry because, at the end of the tour, we learned that Pol Pot died in his sleep at the age of 72. The blood of millions of people was on his hands, and yet he did not face justice for his crimes. Furthermore, in one of his last interviews, he stated that he felt no remorse for his actions and that his conscience was clear. How can this be? Should he not have to pay for his crimes? Did he escape justice?

What should happen to evil people like Pol Pot? Should death be the end? Is death the way in which people pay for their crimes? Is the death of evil people like Pol Pot, Adolf Hitler, Saddam Hussein, and Osama bin Laden true and sufficient justice?

What about all of the people who have committed egregious crimes but have never been found out or caught?

There has been plenty of unsolved and unreported murder, rape, assault, vandalism, fraud, sabotage, thuggery, and a host of other crimes whereby victims have suffered but perpetrators have never been found out. There are people who have never faced justice for their actions precisely because no authority had knowledge of the crime or because those with the knowledge lacked sufficient authority or will to carry out justice.

Should all people everywhere answer for the crimes and offenses they have committed even if the rest of humanity does not know about the offenses? Should every act of evil have to answer to a judge? If we are honest with ourselves, most of us would agree that there must be something greater in terms of punishment for truly evil people. But what would such punishment look like? Who has the power and the right to dispense such justice? Whose definition of evil and justice should we use as we discuss these issues? Who is able to bring true justice in a consistent manner for all people everywhere and in every time period in history?

God is the only being who is uniquely able to determine that which is evil and that which demands judgment or justice. He is the only being who is able to know every thought and action in the entire universe and throughout history. Moreover, He alone has the power and authority over the created order to exercise His justice. Finally, He is the only being who is good, righteous, and perfect and thus willing and able to dispense true justice. Let us consider what the Bible says about God that might explain how He is uniquely qualified to judge the world.

GOD'S PRESENCE AND JUDGMENT

Any being that cannot be fully everywhere at the same time and for all time is not able to bring about cosmic justice. If there is one square mile in creation that a being cannot observe, then that being lacks the ability to be a universally trustworthy judge. Thus no created being is qualified to be the universal judge. Only a being who is omnipresent, omniscient, omnipotent, and eternal can bring about true justice.

The God of the Bible is omnipresent. He is everywhere at all times.[2] And He has been fully and simultaneously everywhere throughout history. In fact, there is no place in creation where God is not fully present. There is no place where someone can go and hide from God. "'Am I a God who is near," declares the LORD, "and not a God far off? Can a man hide himself in hiding places so I do not see him?" declares the LORD. "Do I not fill the heavens and the earth?" declares the LORD' (Jer. 23:23-24).[3] There is no

---

2   Millard J. Erickson, *Christian Theology*, 2nd edition (Grand Rapids: Baker, 1998), 299.

3   Bible references such as 'Jer. 23:23-24' refer to the book called Jeremiah, to the twenty-third chapter of that Bible book, and specifically to the twenty-third and twenty-fourth verses of that

dark corner of the ocean, no deep pocket in the crust of the earth, no millimeter of space in the heavens where God is not (Ps. 139:7-10).

Since God is omnipresent, He has never missed any activity throughout history. He has been present in the most secret meetings of those plotting genocide and in the windowless apartments where the deviant is plotting evil at this very moment. The Bible says that He is everywhere and that His eyes see everything (2 Chron. 16:9). Indeed, God has heard every word that has ever been spoken and will hold people accountable for them: 'I tell you that every careless word that people speak, they shall give an accounting for it in the day of judgment' (Matt. 12:36).

GOD'S KNOWLEDGE AND JUDGMENT

God is also omniscient, or all-knowing. He is everywhere in His creation at all times, and He is able to know all things that have ever happened in the past or will happen in the future: 'There is no creature hidden from His sight, but all things are open and laid bare to the eyes of Him with whom we have to do' (Heb. 4:13). Because He is also an infinitely wise God, He is also able to know all of the thoughts and

---

chapter. Thus 'bookname xx:yy' refers to chapter xx, verse yy of the book by that name. Most versions of the Bible have a table of contents with page numbers to help readers locate each book by name. Unless otherwise indicated, biblical quotations are taken from the New American Standard Bible or NASB (Anaheim, CA: Foundation Publications, 1995).

intentions in the hearts and minds of all creatures everywhere (Pss. 44:21; 139:4; 147:5; 1 John 3:20).[4] Thus God knows all of the actions, intentions, thoughts, and detailed desires of every person throughout the universe at this very moment.

God is not merely a transcendent God who knows all things at a distance, like a cosmic supercomputer. He is also a God who is uniquely involved with His creation and knows every single thing about all of His creatures. He knows and numbers every hair on every head (Matt. 10:30). He knows each word on the tips of our tongues long before we even speak (Ps. 139:4). He knows us completely, and on an intimate level: 'Do not worry then, saying, "What will we eat?" or "What will we drink?" or "What will we wear for clothing?" For the Gentiles eagerly seek all these things; for your heavenly Father knows that you need all these things. But seek first His kingdom and His righteousness, and all these things will be added to you' (Matt. 6:31-33).

God also knows and ordains all future events, actions, intentions, and desires for all created beings: He 'declares the end from the beginning, and from ancient times things which have not been done, saying, "My purpose will be established, and I will accomplish all My good pleasure"' (Isa. 46:10). All things are laid bare before God, and He

---

4   Wayne Grudem, *Systematic Theology: An Introduction to Biblical Doctrine* (Grand Rapids: Zondervan, 1994), 190.

knows all things truly (Heb. 4:13). God cannot be deceived or convinced that an action was good when it was actually evil. He knows everything that has ever been and ever will be, and thus stands as the only being who is able to judge and administer true justice for all people everywhere.

God's Power and Judgment

A god or being who lacks complete sovereign authority over all creation is not capable of bringing the vilest offenders to justice. If a being lacked the power to bring one single person or angel to justice, then that being would lack the supremacy to dispense true justice. Thus, any being who is ruler over only a portion or aspect of creation is not able to bring cosmic justice.

The God of the Bible is truly omnipotent, or all-powerful.[5] He does not merely rule or establish the rule over a portion of the creation. He is the sovereign Lord who created all things and is thus authoritative over His handiwork. Since He alone is the Creator of all that has ever been created, He alone has sovereign authority over creation. He is the Almighty God (2 Cor. 6:18) who can establish the stars in the sky and decree their actions (Gen. 1; Ps. 147:4).

He establishes nations, raises them up for seasons, and brings them low, all in accordance with His divine plans (Exod. 32:10). God has authority over every single nation

---

5   Erickson, *Christian Theology*, 302.

and the rulers of those nations (Ps. 2). He has authority over all creation and is the only being capable of upholding true justice.

All humans will give an account to their omnipotent Creator. All angels and powers will give an account to Him. When God decides to bring all things before Him to give an account for their actions, they will obey His sovereign rule and submit to the judgment He deems right (Isa. 66).

GOD'S ETERNALITY AND JUDGMENT

God is eternal. He existed before the foundation of the world and the existence of time (Eph. 1:3-9). He is eternal going backward, in terms of the past. There has never been a moment inside of creation or prior to creation in which He was not in full existence. He is the 'Everlasting God' whose years cannot be counted, because years cannot contain a fraction of God's eternality (Job 36:26; Isa. 40:28). He alone has never had a beginning.

God is also eternal moving forward, in terms of the future. There will never be a moment in the future in which He will not fully exist. He is the God 'who is and who was and who is to come' (Rev. 1:8). God has neither beginning nor end; He is eternal.

Because God is eternal, He is uniquely qualified to judge all created things. He was before creation, has fully existed during the history of creation, and will exist in the future.

Therefore, in conjunction with His omnipresence and omniscience, we can know that God has never missed an event in any place in creation. He does not have to rely on a secondary witness in order to judge His creatures, as He has been omnipresent and omniscient through eternity past and into eternity future. He is the only being who has been and will be everywhere at all times, and there will never be a moment or event He overlooks. His eternality combined with His unchanging nature (see 'immutability' below) helps us to understand that He will apply the same standard of judgment at the beginning of time as well as at the end of time. In other words, God's eternality (in conjunction with His other attributes) helps us to trust His judgments. There is no other being like God. All other beings are limited in some capacity that infringes upon their ability to judge in the same manner that God does. If justice is to be obtained, only an omnipresent, omnipotent, and eternal God is qualified to bring it about.

GOD'S IMMUTABILITY AND JUDGMENT

God is immutable, which means that He does not and cannot change.[6] He has always been the same and will continue to be so throughout eternity. Psalm 102:25-27 says: 'Of old You founded the earth, and the heavens are the work of Your hands. Even they will perish, but You endure;

---

6   Ibid., 305.

and all of them will wear out like a garment; like clothing You will change them and they will be changed. But You are the same, and Your years will not come to an end.'

God does not grow, mature, or change in any capacity. He is consistent, and His nature and character do not change. His love at the beginning of time is the same love He will possess in the future. His disposition toward evil will never change. He will not become complacent toward wickedness. His attitude toward murder will always be as it was in eternity past.

In a world of ever-evolving technologies, where newer is better, it seems counterintuitive that an eternal God, who never changes or is updated, could be greater than all things. In our society, things that are upgraded or changed are generally improved for the better. This means that their previous versions were lacking in some capacity that is fixed with a new update. My new iPhone is less than a month old, yet I have already installed two updates. Theoretically, each update makes the phone and its capacities better than the previous version. But God does not change, because He is perfect and does not need to change. He cannot get better in any manner, since everything that He is and does is already perfect. There will never be a God 2.0 like there will be an iOS 20.0. He cannot be upgraded, because perfection will always be perfection.

We can take great comfort in knowing that God is perfect and unchanging. We can know that He has never lied, cheated, acted in the wrong, or committed any crime. We can find consolation in knowing that He is perfectly righteous and will never act in any way that will lessen or demean His righteousness. This means that He always acts in the right. And because His actions are always right, we can trust that God's judgments are always right. Psalm 119:137 says: 'Righteous are You, O Lord, and upright are Your judgments.'

In other words, God is the only being who is able to make right judgments and bring about perfect justice because of who He is. He is eternal and omnipresent and therefore cannot miss a single thing. He will never blink or turn His head so that something occurs outside of His knowledge. He is omniscient and knows all actions, thoughts, and intentions of every creature that has ever lived. He alone has seen every righteous act and every evil deed. He is also perfect and unchanging, so that His standards are constant and unmoving. God is all-powerful and therefore able to bring to justice every vile person whose actions, thoughts, and intentions are worthy of judgment. He is righteous and therefore fair in His judgments. He will never judge wrongly or be overly harsh, because His own nature keeps Him from such mistakes.

When God carries out universal justice through judgment, we should not see Him as ruthless or vile. Rather, as I will argue in this book, we should see Him as a loving God who cares for right and wrong. Because God is who He is, the Pol Pots and Saddam Husseins of the world will never get away with evil. In fact, no evil thought or action will go unpunished precisely because God is the One who judges and makes all things right.

HOW WILL GOD PUNISH THE GUILTY?

The Bible says that God will make a just judgment between the innocent and the guilty. It also says that all who are pronounced guilty will be sentenced to an eternity in hell. Hell is the place where God will pour out His divine wrath on the guilty for eternity future.

For many of us, we still have questions and concerns about God and hell. The following chapters consider such fundamental questions as:

- *Chapter 2: If God sends anyone to hell, can He still be loving?*
- *Chapter 3: Would a loving Jesus send anyone to hell?*
- *Chapter 4: What do the loving apostles say about hell?*
- *Chapter 5: Is there a way in which guilty people can avoid hell?*
- *Chapter 6: Is hell eternal?*
- *Chapter 7: Will hell be emptied at some point?*
- *Chapter 8: Conclusion*
- *Appendix: Frequently Asked Questions*

2

How Can a Loving God Send Anyone to Hell?

On January 24, 2018, world-renowned sports doctor Larry Nassar was sentenced to between 40 and 175 years in prison by Judge Rosemarie Aquilina. How can a judge sentence a person to 175 years in prison and call it justice? Was Judge Aquilina being too heavy-handed? When she pronounced the sentence to Nassar, she said, 'I've just signed your death warrant. I find that you don't get it. You are still a danger.' [1] Why would a judge feel as though justice was being served with this long prison sentence?

Before we answer this question, we should consider some of Dr Nassar's crimes. Over 150 individuals came forward

---

1   Eric Levenson, 'Larry Nassar Sentenced to up to 175 Years in Prison for Decades of Sexual Abuse', *CNN*, Cable News Network, 25 Jan. 2018, www.cnn.com/2018/01/24/us/larry-nassar-sentencing/index.html.

in his trial to report that they had been sexually assaulted by the Michigan State University doctor over the course of two decades. He used his position of power and authority to exploit and continuously assault his victims. Furthermore, Nassar did not demonstrate much remorse but instead felt justified in his actions. In a letter he wrote to the court, he stated: 'I was a good doctor because my treatments worked, and those patients that are now speaking out are the same ones that praised me and came back over and over. The media convinced them that everything I did was wrong and bad. They feel like I broke their trust. Hell hath no fury like a woman scorned.'[2]

Judge Aquilina made her judgment based on the heinous nature and the sheer multitude of the crimes that Nassar committed against his victims, as well as the fact that he seemed quite unrepentant. It is clear that Nassar has caused great pain to a vast number of people, and he deserves to be punished. Was Judge Aquilina's sentence unloving? Or did she act in a manner that is a type of justice to society? When Nassar's sentence was read, there was a sense of great relief in the courtroom, as many of the doctor's victims thanked the judge for upholding justice. In other words, far from being unloving, Judge Aquilina will be remembered for standing up for justice. Perhaps this type of court case can help us think through the question we face in this chapter.

---

2   Ibid.

How can a loving God send anyone to hell? Those who ask this question are not alone. Before we can begin to explore an answer, let us open up our question a bit to see what is behind it. If we work through the question and some of the assumptions behind it, maybe our specific answers will have greater meaning.

First, we may tend to work from our own definition of love. In fact, it is possible that the question itself displays one's current feeling on the matter. In other words, one might be thinking, if God sends *anyone* to hell, then obviously He is not all-loving. If He were all-loving, He would not send anyone to hell. We tend to see God's love in one category, with one result: A loving God loves all people equally and would never punish a single person. Therefore, if there is someone in hell, then God is not loving. Perhaps the question is more accurately framed, 'Shouldn't God's love trump His holiness?'

Second, we may tend to think that most people who might end up in hell do not deserve to be there. Most of us tend to see the vast majority of humanity as, generally speaking, 'good'. We can admit that all people are guilty of lying, cheating, stealing, hating, having impure thoughts, coveting, and being selfish. But these are just part of being human, right? Surely these things are not worthy of being called 'sins' that would land someone in hell for eternity. In other words, many people that Christians say are in hell may be viewed, from our vantage point, as decent and not worthy of that dreadful place. Perhaps the question should be framed, 'Most people are good, so why does God want to punish them at all?'

In order to answer the main question of this chapter, we will attempt to understand a few more characteristics of God and our human condition in light of God (as we did in the first chapter). This is a 'top-down' move that gives us a consistent and stable starting point. If we do not start with God and work down toward humanity, we might end up in a situation in which we cannot find any agreeable ground from which any universal answers can be given (one of the difficulties of postmodernity). Therefore, we will examine aspects of the character of God (including His independence, holiness, love, righteousness, and unity), of humanity and the human condition, and of the type of punishment (if any) we deserve for sinning against God.

WHO IS GOD? HIS ATTRIBUTES SHOW US WHO AND WHAT HE IS

GOD IS INDEPENDENT

The Bible portrays God as an independent being who is complete in Himself and needs nothing because He lacks nothing.[3] He exists because He is God and does not owe

---

3   Wayne Grudem, *Systematic Theology*, 160-1.

His existence to anything or anyone. He is not bound to anyone's demands of Him, for He is complete and prior to anything else. He is the 'I Am Who I Am', the God who is, who was, and who will be (Exod. 3:14). This 'I Am' God was, is, and will be completely perfect and lacking in nothing throughout His eternal existence.

Since this independent God is perfectly complete, He does not need anything, and nothing can make Him more or less than what He is already: 'The God who made the world and all things in it, since He is Lord of heaven and earth, does not dwell in temples made with hands; nor is He served by human hands, as though He needed anything, since He Himself gives to all people life and breath and all things' (Acts 17:24-25). There is not a single thing that God needs. He cannot become greater or more glorious than He already is, was, and will be.

Furthermore, He is the primary cause of all things in the universe, and all things flow from Him and are for Him. When He creates, He does so because He desires to create. He does not do so in order to fill something lacking in Him. He is not lonely or in need of fellowship, since He is perfect and complete in Himself.

God is infinite, and we are finite. He is eternal, and we are not. He is perfect in all of His ways and understanding. We are human and tend to misunderstand and misrepresent things. In light of these truths, as well as the fact that God is before us and the One to whom we owe our existence, we do not get to select God's attributes or define what they mean. In His perfection, He gets to define Himself as He is, and He will create the meaning of the terms and images He uses to describe Himself.

Therefore, when the Bible says that God is *something*, He gets to define what that *something* is. When He gives us a picture or an image that helps us to understand Him better, He gets to articulate how He relates to His creation through that image. Our best way to understand God as He is (to the extent finite creatures can understand the infinite God) will always be as we allow God to define Himself and give us the meaning behind His attributes as seen through the Bible.

We tend to distort our understanding of God and our world when we try to make God answer to *our* definitions of who He is or of one of His attributes. In other words, when we define God's love with our own definition of love, we create errors in our thinking. The same holds true for any of God's attributes. If we try to force God into our notions of these things, we are revealing who *we* desire God to be rather than what *He* has revealed Himself to be. So, as we briefly work through a few more of God's attributes, we will once again examine them from the context of a biblical worldview.

GOD IS HOLY

What does it mean for God to be holy? The Bible tells us that God *is* the definition of holiness (1 Pet. 1:15-16). God is completely separate from sin or the taint of sin and is righteous in all cases at all times.[4] In holiness, God is utterly unique in majesty (Exod. 15:11); He is the very essence of holiness (Isa. 8:13).[5] In other words, God, in His being and in His nature, is holiness. Every action and every thought of God is, by definition, holy. He does not act in any way that is unholy or impure or in a manner that could be rightly defined as sinful or wrong. Since He is completely and eternally perfect in purity and morality, holiness can be understood as the complete absence of sin or any sense of wrongness. Theologian Thomas C. Oden clarifies God's holiness in this way:

> The moral quality that best points to God's incomparably good character, as one incomparable in power, is holiness, for holiness implies that every excellence fitting to the Supreme Being is found in God without blemish or limit. It also implies that all other divine moral excellences (goodness, justice, mercy, truth, and grace) are unified and made mutually harmonious in infinite degree in God.[6]

---

4   Ibid., 201.

5   Erickson, *Christian Theology*, 311.

6   Thomas C. Oden, *The Living God: Systematic Theology, Volume One* (Peabody, MA: Prince, 1987), 99.

The book of Isaiah refers to God as 'holy, holy, holy' (Isa. 6:1-3). Not only does this threefold repetition signify that God is perfectly holy; it also indicates that He is utterly unique in His holiness, as no other creature or being can share in this exact capacity of holiness. Hosea 11:9 says concerning God: 'For I am God and not man—the Holy One in your midst.' There is none like this God. He is holy and will always act in a manner consistent with His perfect holiness. He will never make a mistake or treat any creature in a manner unbecoming to His holiness. His treatment of all creatures will be right and true.

Second, the Bible also says: 'It is the LORD of hosts whom you should regard as holy. And He shall be your fear, And He shall be your dread' (Isa. 8:13). The reason we are to dread and fear this holy God is because we are not holy. We are creatures who violate God's laws and commandments in our actions and thoughts. We are sinners against God and should understand that His holiness demands He act against sin and those who commit sin. If we ever have a view of God that does not lead us to a right and proper fear of Him, we do not have a biblical view of God. We are to fear Him precisely because He is perfectly holy and will not tolerate any hint of imperfection, impurity, or sin. In fact, according to God's holiness, He must punish sin. In other words, because He *is* holy and we are sinful, His nature and essence demand that He carry out punishment against sinners.

When we think through how God *should* punish sin, we tend to stop far short of seeing this issue from God's perspective. We see it from our own vantage point of those who are sinful, and, truthfully, we simply desire that He not punish us for our sin. In other words, we are hoping that God will 'turn off' His holiness and just be pure love (in our conception) so that He will not punish us. However, God will not set aside His holiness in order to carry out His love (since the two attributes work in harmony with one another and not against one another). His holy nature demands that He act against all sin and impurity with judgment. Furthermore, due to God's independence, He cannot be swayed in His judgments. He does not *need* to have our approval or agreement when He judges sin. He judges sin because He is holy.

GOD IS LOVE

When we say, 'God is love', what do we mean? We tend to think that God's love means He is equally benevolent to all people, all things, at all times. But is this divine love? It seems that if God loves all things equally, then He does not love anything truly.[7] If He loves Saddam Hussein and cancer in the same way He loves us, then there is nothing unique or special about His love and concern for you or me. In other

---

7 For a helpful essay on God's love see D. A. Carson, 'Distorting the Love of God?' in Christopher W. Morgan (ed.), *The Love of God*, (Wheaton, IL: Crossway, 2016), 21-32.

words, universally equal benevolence is not love, no matter how appealing the notion might sound.

A helpful analogy is the love that is unique within the confines of a monogamous marriage. A husband and wife should possess a love for one another that neither party shares with another person. Hopefully, the husband loves his wife in a way that he does not love his brother's wife, a complete stranger, or any other woman that he meets. In fact, some marriages are torn apart when one member of the marriage commits adultery with someone else. Real love tends to have a context, limitations, and consequences for failure to love rightly.

If we are to discern God's love and how it is displayed, we must look to the Bible to see how God has defined love for Himself. First, God *is* love (1 John 4:8). This means not that God is only loving at times and does lovely things but that He *is* love. God is the definition of love, and therefore everything He does is somehow characterized by His love. Timothy George captures God's perfect Trinitarian[8] love in this passage: '[Trinitarian love] refers to the fact that from all eternity the God of the Bible has known himself as a sweet society of three divine persons—the Father, the Son, and

---

8   'Trinity' is a term that defines God as one God who has revealed Himself in three persons: the Father, the Son, and the Holy Spirit. All three persons in the Trinity are distinct and yet without division in nature, being, or essence.

the Holy Spirit—freely united in the reciprocity of their uncoerced love for one another.'[9]

In other words, God is love, and His love is demonstrated perfectly in the unity of the Trinity. The Father perfectly loves the Son and Holy Spirit, and vice versa. God's love is not merely a feeling or an emotion. Rather, it is a perfect commitment to something. The Bible says that the Father loves the Son and that the Son loves the Father (John 3:35). This means that the Father's love toward the Son is a driving commitment that cannot be broken or disturbed. The Son of God so loves the Father that He will perfectly carry out the will and plan of the Father.

The Bible also says that God loves people of the world (John 3:16). This means that God has a beautiful commitment to the people He has created. However, we cannot think for a moment that God's love will ever violate His holiness. In fact, we should see God's love as working in concert with His perfect holiness and never outside of or pitted against it.[10]

God is love. God is holy. God is independent. These attributes manifest themselves in ways that are consistent

---

9   Timothy George, 'The Doctrine of God: The Nature of God: Being, Attributes, and Acts', in Daniel L. Akin (ed.) *A Theology for the Church*, (Nashville: B&H, 2007), 226.

10   Ibid., 225.

with each other rather than against one another.[11] Thus, the God who *is* love will punish sin, and He will do so in a manner that does not break or compromise His holiness. It is in this way that God's love, as it is carried out in holiness and justice, is perfect regardless of how we might think of it. In other words, God's judgment against sin and sinners is not only holy but also loving (according to God's definition of love).

As sinful people, we tend to manipulate one another through our withholding of love. When we desire to punish people, we withhold our love and affection from them until they come around to our way of thinking. In other words, we tend to sulk until the other person acquiesces to our view. This is not really love in action but rather manipulation. While this childish behavior might work with other fallen humans, it cannot work with God. His independence tells us that He does not *need* our love or approval. He certainly demands it, but He cannot be manipulated into moving from His holiness in order to come to our way of thinking.

Therefore, when we think that a loving God should not punish sin, we are not thinking rightly. That type of thinking is a love without any sort of holiness attached to it. In fact, that type of love is not really love. Rather, it seems more like an unrealistic hope not centered on goodness.

---

11 Michael Horton, *The Christian Faith: A Systematic Theology for Pilgrims on the Way* (Grand Rapids: Zondervan, 2011), 266.

Would a *loving* God punish sin? Yes, and He will do so. Would a *loving* God send someone to hell for his or her sins? Yes, and the loving God of the Bible will do so, because His love is consistent with His other attributes. A divine love that distorts God's holiness is not true love. Besides, God cannot and will not allow any injustice to go unpunished.

GOD IS RIGHTEOUS

When we ask the question, 'How can a loving God send anyone to hell?' are we implying that God is being unfair or unjust? *Is* God unfair? Is there a chance that God acts in an unrighteous manner? Can some of God's actions be declared unjust? Should God ever allow injustice to go unpunished? Will He ever reward evil?

The Bible declares that God is righteous and just: 'The Rock! His work is perfect, for all His ways are just; A God of faithfulness and without injustice, Righteous and upright is He' (Deut. 32:4); 'Righteousness and justice are the foundation of His throne' (Ps. 97:2). These things necessarily flow together with God's holiness and love as He interacts with His creation. Millard Erickson says that God's righteousness is 'God's holiness applied to his relationships to other beings. The righteousness of God means, first of all, that the law of God, being a true expression of his nature, is as perfect as he is… The righteousness of God also means that his actions are in accord with the law he himself has established.'[12] God does not merely do things that are right, although He does. Rather, God is the *definition* of righteousness and justice. In other words, *righteous* and *just* find their correct definitions in what God does. Therefore, by definition, all of God's actions are righteous and just in all situations at all times, because He is holy and will never act in a manner that is unholy, unfair, unjust, or unrighteous.

Moreover, as our Creator, God also defines what is and is not right and just for us. Not only does He possess the authority to do so, but what is right and just is seen in His nature and goodness. His standards are *the* standards for the entire world. Furthermore, when we reflect on God's righteousness in light of His immutability, we can know that God's working of righteousness will never change. His standards will never change or alter in the slightest. Because His righteousness and justice will always be the same, consistent throughout history, even in judgment, He cannot be charged with being unjust. His standards and punishment against sin will never change. He will never grow accustomed to sin or allow it to tarnish His holiness.

Because God is righteous and just, He will punish sin. When confronted with any sin, God will always provide true justice in a righteous manner as He punishes. He will never be more or less severe than the situation demands;

---

12 Erickson, *Christian Theology*, 313.

perfect justice will be carried out at all times. God is also the One who determines who has violated His laws, and He gets to determine what the right and just punishment is for those crimes.

GOD IS UNITY

Can God 'turn off' some of His attributes in order to carry out a task? No, God is all of His attributes all of the time, and that type of behavior would not only be contrary to His character, it would also be a violation of His nature. Everything that He does is from and through all of His attributes in sync with one another. Thus He is 100 percent of all His attributes simultaneously in every single action and thought. He will never act in love outside of holiness or righteousness. Nor will He act in holiness outside of His love. God will always act in a manner consistent with all of His attributes at the same time.

In light of these truths, let us consider our question again: 'How can a loving God send anyone to hell?' We know that God is holy and will always act in a manner that results in perfect holiness. He is unchanging, as are His standards. God is love and His love is consistent with His holiness and will never violate holiness or justice. He cannot be coerced and will never be manipulated into anything contrary to His own character or nature.

Thus, if in our question we are implying that God is not loving because He executes judgment against sin, then we understand neither God nor love. Furthermore, if we understand these things rightly yet continue to ask God not to punish sin, we are actually seeking a portion of injustice to be allowed in God's world. This cannot happen, because God is just, righteous, good, fair, loving, and holy. He will always act in perfect accordance with all of His attributes at all times. Perhaps Christopher Morgan and Robert Peterson are correct when they reframe the question of our book from 'How could a loving God send anyone to hell?' to 'How could a just and holy God ever declare guilty sinners to be righteous in his sight?'[13] In other words, what kind of a god would God be if He allowed sin to go unpunished?

THE HUMAN CONDITION

I like the people in my neighborhood. They are kind and quite considerate. When I drive by as they are out walking their dogs, we smile and wave to one another. When the Santa Ana winds of Southern California exceed 50 mph, my neighbors are more than willing to help me collect my garbage cans when they have fallen over and littered the street. While I do not know every detail about them, my neighbors seem, on the surface, to be good and decent people. It is

---

13 Christopher W. Morgan and Robert A. Peterson, *What is Hell?* Basics of Faith (Phillipsburg, NJ: P&R, 2010), 8.

hard to see myself, or them, as being *so bad* that we deserve God's eternal punishment. Perhaps there is something I am missing. Either they are worse than I thought (it might be time to move!) or else I am not seeing them (or myself) in the same light that God does. As we consider who we are as human beings, we must remember that we come from God. He is our source, and we owe our entire being to Him. If we do not see ourselves in light of our Creator, then we will make incorrect assumptions at every turn.

WE ARE CREATED BY GOD[14]

According to the Bible, the eternal, loving, holy, righteous, and just God has created all creation. In Genesis 1, God speaks the universe into existence. It is apparently a mature creation that is fully functional and has the appearance of age. Plants and animals are already able to reproduce after their own kinds (Gen. 1:24). Adam and Eve, though they have no human parents, are created fully mature and able to carry out the functions of reproduction, work, and worship.

Furthermore, because God is the Creator of the universe, everything inside of His creation must operate within His designated structures. The sun and the moon do not chart their own courses but rather rule the sky on God's behalf exactly as He has declared they should (Gen. 1:14-16). The

---

14 The categories in this section come from Christopher W. Morgan, *Christian Theology: The Biblical Story and Our Faith* (Nashville, B&H Academic: forthcoming).

waters of the oceans and the seas are at God's beck and call and carry out His plans for them (Ps. 89:9). Animals do what they do precisely because God is their Creator and has given them purpose. He has told the creatures, 'Be fruitful and multiply, and fill the waters in the seas and let birds multiply on the earth' (Gen. 1:22). To each aspect of creation God has given instruction and instinct that compel them.

He has not created merely to see what creation will do without a sense of direction. Rather, He creates and gives order and instruction for His creation so that it functions as He has designed it to function. As the created order functions as God has determined, it carries out right actions in obedience to His commands. This obedience is, in a manner, a type of righteousness (or being in the right as it pertains to God and His commands). Anything less than obedience to God's commands and laws is a failure to obey, or sin.

WE ARE CREATED IN THE IMAGE OF GOD

The Bible also tells us that humanity is God's crown jewel of creation. God creates mankind in His own image: 'Let Us make man in Our image, according to Our likeness' (Gen. 1:26). Being made in God's image means that humans have something that the rest of creation does not. This uniqueness comes in the fact that we have souls and have a governing responsibility back to God. Much like the sun and the moon 'rule' the day and the night, so humanity has the obligation to 'rule'. We are called to rule and be good stewards over the creatures in the waters, in the air, on land, and even across the earth as a whole (Gen. 1:26). This rule, or governing, means that humanity is charged with a special purpose that belongs to us and us alone. As those who are created in His image, humanity is entrusted by God with this task of ruling and caring for His creation.

WE ARE GOD'S IMAGE-BEARERS CREATED TO LOVE AND SERVE GOD

However, just as the rest of creation must operate as God commands, humanity must also live and operate exactly as God commands. Since God has given us these responsibilities, we should rule or govern according to His nature and character. In other words, all of our actions must necessarily reflect the God who made us in His image and gave us this responsibility. Since God is holy, righteous, just, and loving at the same time, as we image God our actions and interactions with creation must reflect our Creator God. To accomplish this task rightly is to obey God.

Moreover, since we owe our existence back to the Creator God, as God's creatures we should *desire* to live our lives as His proper image-bearing representatives. Right imaging of God in the created order is one way of serving God, and the manner in which we carry it out should display the love and devotion we have for our Creator. This is not something we should *have to do* but rather something we should *want to do*.

WE HAVE FAILED TO IMAGE GOD RIGHTLY

If we live, interact, worship, or rule in any manner that misrepresents God's character or will, we are in violation of God's commands. This misrepresentation is called sin.

Our forefather Adam was called to be God's image-bearer in the garden of Eden. He was told to guard and keep the garden as God's sacred space. He was to keep any unclean thing of the field from entering the clean garden (Gen. 2:15). Specifically, God told him that his food was all of the bountiful and lush trees and plants in the entire garden, except one: 'From any tree of the garden you may eat freely; but from the tree of the knowledge of good and evil you shall not eat, for in the day that you eat from it you will surely die' (vv. 16-17). To obey God's commands would have been an act of righteousness and in right accordance with Adam's responsibilities as God's image-bearer.

The Bible records how Adam failed to obey God, however, and instead sinned as he ate from the tree of the knowledge of good and evil (Gen. 3:6). The Bible also tells us how God responded to Adam in holiness, justice, righteousness, and love. God did not allow sin to go unpunished. He banished

Adam and Eve from the garden and into the field, as they were no longer perfect image-bearers for God (Gen. 3:23-24).

In this punishment, we tend to see God's actions as displaying condemnation and wrath. However, what we often fail to see is God's love on display in perfect accordance with His holiness. God's holy nature could have demanded that Adam and Eve be put to death for their treason against God and His laws. After all, 'the wages of sin is death' (Rom. 6:23). Death is what they deserved, and God would have been righteous in demanding it. However, instead of instant physical death, God sent them out of His immediate localized presence and into the world. But He did not send them out without hope. The Bible is clear to show us that God covered them with the skin of an animal (Gen. 3:21). We are left to assume that the first death of any creature in this world was God's doing. He seemingly ended the life of an animal in order to cover Adam and Eve. This action shows how God can uphold justice and show grace and love at the same time. It also might be a foreshadowing of how God would create a loving system whereby sinful human beings could be allowed back into God's sacred space and avoid His wrath and punishment through the substitutionary work of another. Yet this system will never violate His holiness but instead will still punish sin and sinners (see chapter 5).

WE ALL POSSESS FALLEN SIN NATURES

Because God is always true to His word, there is a type of death that Adam—and, from him, all of humanity—undergoes. As soon as Adam broke God's laws, he received a fallen sin nature. This fallen nature changed everything. It is a nature of death. In fact, the Bible calls people who are in their fallen sin natures 'dead in your trespasses and sins' (Eph. 2:1). This means that, in this nature, no image-bearer can represent God correctly and will therefore always be in the act of sin as humans are in open rebellion against God and His rule. The Bible calls this living and walking in the flesh.

In the flesh, the human mind is contrary to, hostile toward, and at war with God and His ways (Rom. 8:7). We no longer desire to rule or express dominion in the way God requires. We gladly assume that God is wrong and that we are right in our perceptions and judgments. Paul says in Romans 8:7: 'Because the mind set on the flesh is hostile toward God; for it does not subject itself to the law of God, for it is not even able to do so.' The human mind is so depraved that it does not see God's laws rightly and therefore cannot subject itself rightly to God's laws. Moreover, Paul says that the human mind is no longer capable of doing so and will therefore always be in open rebellion against God, and 'those who are in the flesh cannot please God' through obedience to Him (v. 8). This means that all human beings everywhere will live in their sin and trespasses, at war with the holy God.

The Bible teaches: 'The Lord saw that the wickedness of man was great on the earth, and that every intent of the thoughts of his heart was only evil continuously. The Lord was sorry that He had made man on the earth, and He was grieved in His heart' (Gen. 6:5). God was grieved because Adam's fall placed all of humanity in a position of sin and wrath against God. It is no wonder that Paul says that those in this position are 'by nature, children of God's wrath' (Eph. 2:3), as 'there is none righteous, not even one; there is none who understands, there is none who seeks for God…There is none who does good, there is not even one' (Rom. 3:10-12). We are outlaws living in God's world. We live contrary to His law, to His rule, and gladly distort the things He declares to be good and right (Rom. 1–2). In other words, seen from God's correct perspective, 'good people' do not exist.[15] Therefore, all human beings everywhere should be on the receiving end of God's judgment.

GOD'S PUNISHMENT TO ALL SINNERS

We know for a fact that God is holy, righteous, and just. We also know that He will carry out universal justice against those of us who are at war with Him. He will punish sin

---

15 While there certainly are nice people in the world, the Bible describes all people (nice or otherwise) as sinners who are against God and His perfect laws.

and sinners who are dead in their trespasses. The Bible is clear that 'the wages of sin is death' (Rom. 6:23). God will not neglect this punishment, as that would mean allowing cosmic rebellion and injustice to reign in His world.

What is God's ultimate punishment? What is the place where God will carry out His final justice? The Bible calls this place hell. God will be perfectly just, fair, righteous, holy, and loving in His sentencing and punishment. In this way we answer the question posed in this chapter: How can a loving God send anyone to hell? The answer is that the loving God of the Bible does so in order to uphold universal justice. If He allows crimes to go unpunished, He has violated His own holy and righteous nature. But we will also see how God, in perfect concert with His holiness, graciously creates a means of escape from hell as an act of pure love (chapter 5).

Before we get to the good news of God's loving means of escape, we will consider two questions: What does the loving Jesus teach about hell, and what do the loving apostles teach about hell?

3

What Does the Loving Jesus Teach About Hell?

Jesus is known as one of the most loving people ever to live on this earth. His actions in His life prove this fact over and over again. He seeks out those who are cast out by their societies. He spends time with lepers who have been left without human contact. He performs signs and wonders in order to restore those who are broken. He helps the poor and chastises those who ignore this important group. In short, the Bible demonstrates His unfathomable love.

In Matthew 8:1-4 a large crowd gathers around Jesus, including a leper. Leprosy in the Old Testament was a serious disease that often left the leper outside of the city without much human contact. Full-on leprosy has several side effects on the person. If the condition is serious, poor blood supply can lead to one's face being so swollen that it begins to look like a lion's. The disease can also lead to fingers and toes falling off the body. The leper's body also emits a foul odor that can be smelled from a short distance away. In some cases the leper's voice can also take on a harshness and sound quite hoarse.[1] For these reasons and more, in Jesus' day many people simply left lepers to themselves.

But this passage shows Jesus reaching out and touching the leper. Not only does this touch show love and compassion to one who may not have been touched for years; Jesus also heals this man and makes him clean. Jesus heals the leprosy and has the man present himself to the priests in order to prove that the disease is gone so that he can be fully restored to the community that has ostracized him.

Few people would take this kind of risk. But the loving Jesus of Nazareth is more than willing. This fits with His teaching on love for other people: 'In everything, therefore, treat people the same way you want them to treat you, for this is the Law and the Prophets' (Matt. 7:12); 'I tell you, love your enemies and pray for those who persecute you' (5:44). The New Testament is filled with these types of narratives that display the pure love of Jesus. He is known for commanding His followers to love their neighbors as

---

1   This description of lepers is from William Hendriksen and Simon J. Kistemaker, *Exposition of the Gospel According to Matthew*, The New Testament Commentary Series (Grand Rapids: Baker, 1953–2001), 388.

themselves. He is also known for standing up for the poor and denouncing the actions of those who tread upon the less fortunate. Jesus is also seen as loving when He stands up for marginalized women in a man-centered culture. Even if some wonder if He really is the Messiah or if He has risen from the dead, virtually everyone recognizes that Jesus is one of the most loving people in all of history.

Have you ever wondered what this loving Jesus says about hell? Is it possible that He denounces it? What if He does not denounce it but rather affirms its existence and gives details about what it looks like and how long it lasts? Before we examine Jesus' teaching on hell, however, we must first remind ourselves of who He is and has claimed to be. Once we understand who Jesus is, His teachings ought to have a greater impact on us.

WHO IS THIS LOVING JESUS?

JESUS: GOD THE SON

The Bible says that Jesus is the divine Son of God and has the same nature as God the Father: '[Jesus] is the radiance of [God's] glory and the exact representation of His nature and upholds all things by the word of His power' (Heb. 1:3). The Gospel of John begins by identifying Jesus as God: 'In the beginning was the Word and the Word was with God and the Word was God' (John 1:1). This Word who was God was Jesus of Nazareth: 'And the Word became flesh and dwelt among us, and we saw His glory, glory as of the only begotten from the Father, full of grace and truth' (John 1:14). Philippians 2:6 says that Jesus was in the form of God and was God. Colossians 2:9 (ESV) states: 'In [Jesus] the whole fullness of deity dwells bodily.' The Bible is clear that Jesus is fully divine as the Son of God.[2]

It is not merely others in the Bible who claim that Jesus is God, for Jesus Himself makes these claims. He says: 'If you have seen Me then you have seen the Father' (John 14:9), and even utilizes the divine name *Yahweh* (meaning 'I am') in reference to Himself: 'Truly, truly, I say to you, before Abraham was born, I am' (John 8:58; cf. Exod. 3:14). Jesus admits that He is the Son of God (Luke 22:70) and also says that God's glory is His glory: 'This sickness is not to end in death, but for the glory of God, so that the Son of God may be glorified by it' (John 11:4). In other words, Jesus claims to be God. He does not claim to be God the Father but rather claims to be the second person of the Trinity, God the Son.[3]

Not only does the Bible affirm that Jesus is God, it also insists that, as the Son of God, Jesus retains all of the divine attributes that God the Father possesses. Stephen Wellum

---

2   Donald MacLeod, *The Person of Christ* (Downers Grove, IL: InterVarsity Press, 1998), 79.

3   Stephen J. Wellum, *God the Son Incarnate: The Doctrine of Christ* (Wheaton, IL Crossway, 2016), 189.

rightly states: 'All of the divine attributes that make God who he is and enable him to work as only he does are found in Christ—God the Son incarnate.'[4] Jesus, in His full divinity, is the omnipresent, omnipotent, and omniscient God. Thus all of the divine things that can be said about God the Father can also be said of God the Son. As the Son of God, Jesus is the Creator of the universe: '[Jesus] is the image of the invisible God, the firstborn [pre-eminent one] of all creation. For by Him all things were created, both in the heavens and on the earth, visible and invisible, whether thrones or dominions or rulers or authorities—all things have been created through Him and for Him' (Col. 1:15-16); and 'All things were made through Him, and without Him nothing was made' (John 1:3). These passages claim that Jesus was and is the Creator of all that has ever been created. He is the Creator of the universe, the seas, the oceans, the mountains, and all humanity. There is nothing created that He did not create. He created the angels and those angels who would fall, such as Lucifer, or Satan. Moreover, even those realms that cannot be seen at the moment—namely, heaven and hell—have also been created by the Son of God. For our discussion, we need to know that Jesus is the Creator of heaven and all that it entails. But He is also the Creator of hell and everything that it entails.

---

4   Ibid., 192.

Jesus is also the sovereign Son of God who powerfully holds all of His creation together: 'He is before all things, and in Him all things hold together' (Col. 1:17), and the One who 'upholds the universe by the word of His power' (Heb. 1:3).[5] What does 'holds all things together' mean? God the Son is the divine agent behind the things we observe. Gravity does not merely exist because a law states that it must. Gravity exists precisely because God the Son is actively upholding gravity here on the earth so that we can see that 'what goes up must come down.' We can depend on gravity because God the Son is constantly upholding it at this moment and throughout human history.

Likewise, the physics behind terminal velocity do not come from nothing. We are able to recognize the concept of terminal velocity because the Son of God is ensuring that free-falling objects eventually reach a constant speed. We are able to observe it, record it, and define it because God the Son is constantly upholding all things by the word of His power. He is able to uphold 'all things together' because He is fully God and possesses absolute authority over His creation.

Jesus is also the sovereign Son of God over heaven and hell, upholding them and whatever takes place in them. As we will see below, He is the One who determines those who

---

5   Ibid., 194.

gain entry into heaven and will receive eternal life. At the same time, He is the sovereign Son of God over hell. He will determine who has sinned against God and what judgment each person will receive in hell. In short, not only is Jesus the Creator of hell, He is also the One who holds it together and has authority over it.

How can we know that Jesus is what He says He is? How can we know that Jesus is God? The only way we can be sure is if He is able to do the things that only God can do. In other words, He will know things that a normal person could not know and will do things that normal people cannot do.

JESUS: DIVINE OMNISCIENCE

Only the omniscient God can know all things actual and possible. Since He is the sole Creator of the world and has sovereign authority over every aspect of creation, then God alone is omniscient (see chapter 1). There are several occasions in which the Bible shows the omniscience of Jesus as a proof of His divinity. In Mark 2:1-12 Jesus not only knows what people are thinking but also responds to their inward thoughts: 'Immediately Jesus, aware in His spirit that they were reasoning that way within themselves, said to them, "Why are you reasoning about these things in your hearts?"' (Mark 2:8). Jesus is not merely guessing what someone is thinking; rather, He sees into their souls and understands their thoughts before they are ever uttered vocally. This type of knowing is something that God alone can do. This passage, and others like it, are clearly communicating Jesus' omniscience in order to prove that He is fully divine.

In Luke 6:8 Jesus 'knew what they were thinking' and healed a man with a paralyzed hand as a sign to prove His divinity (see also Luke 11:17; Matt. 22:18; John 2:25). Again, this passage is speaking not to Jesus' ability to read body language or posture but to His divine ability to know these people's thoughts even as they are formed in their minds. Not only is Jesus the divine Son of God who is Creator of the world; He is also Lord over every aspect of His creation. In His divinity, there is nothing the Son of God does not know. If the Father knows it, then so too does the divine Son of God. Since Jesus is fully divine, He is omniscient.

Jesus: The Signs and Wonders that prove His Divinity

The Bible offers the miracles of Jesus as one of the fundamental proofs to understanding who He is and claims to be. In other words, Scripture does not merely show these accounts so that we might think highly of Jesus and His compassion, love, and kindness. Rather, these signs and miracles display the true nature of Jesus as God the Son.

As Creator of the world, God alone has control over it, and it responds to God in a unique manner. Thus, when the Bible is showing Jesus' interactions with the world, it is communicating the same truth over and over again: this Jesus is divine, and He has control over the world He has created.[6]

In Mark 4:35-41 Jesus is with His disciples in a raging storm on the Sea of Galilee. The storm is described as 'a fierce gale of wind' so strong that it is already beginning to sink their boat (v. 37). The disciples, some of whom are commercial fishermen accustomed to rough seas, are panicked and cry out to their leader to do something. 'And [Jesus] got up and rebuked the wind and said to the sea, "Hush, be still." And the wind died down and it became perfectly calm' (v. 39).

This verse is not describing an ordinary man yelling aimlessly at the forces of nature in hopes that God will hear him and respond in kindness. Rather, it is giving us a glimpse into who Jesus *really* is as the omnipotent God. When the wind and the sea hear the voice of Jesus, they hear the authoritative voice of their Creator that called out for them to raise up and rage at times in the Old Testament (Pss. 107:25-26; 135:7; 147:18). At once, both the wind and the sea obey their Creator and quiet themselves, so that the passage can speak of them as 'perfectly calm'. It is ironic that both the wind and the sea understand (figuratively speaking) who Jesus is in His divine nature, but His own

---

6   Ibid., 197.

disciples do not yet grasp this truth fully (although they will do so in time): 'They became very much afraid and said to one another, "Who then is this, that even the wind and the sea obey Him?" (Mark 4:41). The answer is obvious, since the winds and waves do not obey the voice of any mere man. Jesus is the omnipotent Son of God, the Creator and sustainer of nature.

In Luke 5:2-9 Jesus meets His disciples as they are returning from a night of fishing in which they have 'worked hard and caught nothing' (v. 5). Jesus speaks to Peter and tells him to place the fishing nets down into the deep water for a catch. 'When they had done this, they enclosed a great quantity of fish, and their nets began to break,' and their boat began to sink (vv. 6-7). This story is not depicting Jesus as a good fisherman who gets lucky with a fortunate placement of a net. Rather, it is written so that we can catch a glimpse of His divine nature. The same voice who created the fish calls out to them to gather in this one particular fishing net in this one precise location of the sea. In response, the fish gather together and drive themselves into Peter's net. There are so many fish obeying the commands of the Son of God that the nets begin to break (Luke 5:6).

Other miracles highlight Jesus' power and authority over nature and the elements of this world as He turns water into wine (John 2:1-11), feeds the crowd of five thousand (Matt. 14:13-21), and walks on water (Mark 6:45-52). All of these passages are designed to display and substantiate that Jesus really is the divine Son of God who has total authority over the entire created order. His voice is heard and obeyed by nature, people, demons, and even Satan himself.

JESUS: GOD THE SON INCARNATE[7]

At the same time we recognize Jesus as fully God, we must also recognize that Jesus became fully man without losing any of His divinity. In one of the greatest acts of love, the Father sent His Son to become the God-man, or God incarnate: 'The Word became flesh and dwelt among us' (John 1:14). Paul writes: 'When the fullness of time had come, God sent His Son, born of a woman, born under the law, to redeem those under the law, that we might receive the adoption to sonship' (Gal. 4:4-5). The 'fullness of time' indicates that the all-powerful God planned this event from before the foundations of the world in order that His Son would enter the world as the sole means to save people from His own wrath. The Father sent His Son to accomplish for humanity what humanity could not accomplish on its own: salvation for the people of God (see chapter 5)!

When did this event happen? Every year, Christians celebrate and remember this climactic occurrence with the festival called Christmas. Christmas commemorates the

---

7   This title comes from Stephen J. Wellum's book by the same title, *God the Son Incarnate*.

incarnation of Jesus Christ, or the event of God the Son adding humanity to His divinity. Christians sing songs to God because of His divine mercy and grace, such as 'O Holy Night' and 'What Child is This?' The angels of heaven took note of this unique moment and sang of God's love in the incarnation: 'Glory to God in the highest, and on earth peace among men with whom He is pleased' (Luke 2:14). In Jesus the full natures of divinity and humanity are united in the one person of Christ. He is the unique God-man.

JESUS: THE LOVING GOD-MAN

Since Jesus is fully divine, every attribute of God discussed in chapters 1–2 can be said of the person of Christ. Therefore, we are right to call Jesus the most loving person who has ever lived. This is true precisely because He is the incarnate God-man who lives out the definition of God's love. Because God is perfect love in the core of His being, so too is God the Son. Thus all of Jesus' actions can rightly be described as perfectly loving. In fact, His miracles and wonders demonstrate God's love for humanity. When Jesus casts out demons from those who are possessed, He is displaying divine love by restoring people, while at the same time displaying His omnipotence over the powers of darkness. When Jesus heals people of their diseases and illnesses, He is showing the love, care, and concern that God has for His creation precisely because He is God the Son incarnate. When Jesus dies on a cross, He is proving 'For God so loved the world that He gave His only begotten Son that whoever believes in Him shall not perish but have eternal life' (John 3:16). In Jesus, we see the perfect love of God. Thus we are right to say that God's love is fully displayed in the person of Jesus Christ.

JESUS: THE RIGHTEOUS GOD-MAN

But just as God cannot be merely one attribute at any one time, neither can the Son of God. Thus, at the same time that Jesus is living out the definition of love, He is also holy, just, and righteous. He is these things exactly as God the Father is holy, righteous, and just. The Father is not any more or less righteous than Jesus is as God the Son.

When Jesus sees corruption in the temple area, He clears it with righteous indignation. The Gospel of John records how Jesus 'made a scourge of cords, and drove them all out of the temple, with the sheep and the oxen; and He poured out the coins of the money changers and overturned their tables; and to those who were selling the doves He said, "Take these things away; stop making My Father's house a place of business" (John 2:15-16). The righteousness of Jesus is no less than His Father's, as they are equal in justice and holiness.

Because Jesus is the Son of God, we should pay attention to what He says about all things. However, for our purposes we must pay special attention to what Jesus says about hell because He is God. If we are right about Jesus, then He is the Creator of the entire created order, including hell. In other words, Jesus is the world's foremost expert on hell because He created it, upholds it, and has authority over it. He uniquely knows who will be in hell because He is the Judge of the world (John 5:21-30). He knows the events and duration of hell precisely because Jesus is the One who carries out divine punishment there (Rev. 14:9-11). In fact, there is nothing that Jesus does not know about hell, because He is the Son of God who knows all things.

WHAT DID THIS LOVING JESUS BELIEVE AND TEACH ABOUT HELL?

Now that we have considered what the Bible asserts about Jesus' true identity and authority, we can consider what Jesus Himself taught about hell. Jesus' understanding of hell can be summarized under four headings: Hell as punishment, hell as destruction, hell as eternal, and hell as banishment.[8]

---

8   These categories are not original with this book. They can be seen in other books on hell, such as Christopher W. Morgan and Robert A. Peterson, *What is Hell?* Basics of Faith (Phillipsburg, NJ: P&R, 2010); idem., (eds), *Hell Under Fire: Modern Scholarship Reinvents Eternal Punishment* (Grand Rapids: Zondervan, 2004); and Eryl Davies, *An Angry God? What the Bible Says About Wrath, Final Judgment, and Hell* (Bryntirion, Bridgend, Wales: Evangelical Press of Wales, 1991).

HELL AS PUNISHMENT

Divine punishment is the primary picture of hell in the Bible. For this reason, most of the passages on hell are vivid warnings that attempt to dissuade the hearer from ending up there. Jesus warns the crowds that they should address those areas in their lives in which they are guilty before God so that they will not be thrown into hell: 'If your right eye makes you stumble, tear it out and throw it from you; for it is better for you to lose one of the parts of your body, than for your whole body to be thrown into hell' (Matt. 5:29). Jesus is driving home the point that no pain on earth can be likened to that of hell. One must do whatever is necessary in this life to ensure that one is not sentenced to hell for eternity, as the pain will be unbearable.

The punishment of hell is described by Jesus as wailing and gnashing of teeth: 'I say to you that many will come from east and west, and recline at the table with Abraham, Isaac, and Jacob in the kingdom of heaven; but the sons of the kingdom will be cast out into the outer darkness; in that place there will be weeping and gnashing of teeth' (Matt. 8:11-12; see also 22:13; 24:51; 25:30; Luke 13:22-30). The wailing is a vocal response to the total punishment that will come upon all who are sentenced to hell for violating the laws of the infinitely holy and excellent God. The gnashing of teeth is a physical reaction to the same complete punishment as one consciously endures perfect divine wrath and yet maintains one's anger toward God (Acts 7:54). In other words, those in hell are able to feel and endure the pain in hell because they are cognizant and alive.

Jesus also uses the imagery of fire in order to describe the painful reality of hell. He says that those who are guilty of breaking God's laws will be 'liable to the hell of fire' (Matt. 5:22; 7:19). These fires of hell are also described as a 'furnace of fire' in which sinners are consumed and punished by the holy, righteous, and just God (Matt. 13:41-42, 49-50): 'The Son of Man will send forth His angels, and they will gather out of His kingdom all stumbling blocks, and those who commit lawlessness, and will throw them into the furnace of fire; in that place there will be weeping and gnashing of teeth.'

Jesus also tells a parable about a rich man and a beggar named Lazarus. This parable expresses great truth about the pain and suffering of God's judgment. He tells of how a rich man is sent into Hades. There the rich man 'lifted up his eyes, being in torment, and saw Abraham far away and Lazarus in his bosom. And he cried out and said, "Father Abraham, have mercy on me and send Lazarus so that he may dip the tip of his finger in water and cool off my tongue, for I am in agony in this flame"' (Luke 16:23-24). While this is a parable and might not be an exact picture of the pain in hell, it does speak to the nature of punishment, torment, and agony of those who face God's just wrath. The rich man is in torment because he has sinned against the Most Holy God, who is justly punishing him. The torment, while just, is also a conscious pain. The rich man is alive and able to feel the anguish of his punishment. This teaching on Hades seems to be a foreshadowing of the type of fiery punishment that sinners will face in hell.

This imagery of hell as fire coincides with the Old Testament's description of God judging His enemies as an all-consuming fire. This helps us understand passages such as Mark 9:43, where Jesus warns, 'If your hand causes you to stumble, cut it off; it is better for you to enter life crippled, than, having your two hands, to go into hell, into unquenchable fire.' Hell is the place where the wicked will face God's pure and holy wrath as an unquenchable fire. The point of this image is to show that God's just and perfect wrath in hell is a painful reality for the wicked.

HELL AS DESTRUCTION

According to Jesus, hell is not merely a place of punishment but is also a place of destruction. He teaches His disciples about the power of God in judgment as far greater than any power of humanity. He warns, 'Do not fear those who kill the body but are unable to kill the soul; but rather fear Him who is able to destroy both soul and body in hell' (Matt. 10:28). The warning in this passage is clear: to fall into the hands of those who can kill or destroy the body is one thing, but it pales in comparison to falling into the wrath of God, who will eternally destroy His enemies, body and soul, in the consuming fire of hell. This type of destruction will be more painful than one could imagine.

Jesus teaches that hell is the place in which unrepentant sinners will perish in a state of destruction (John 3:16; Matt. 7:13-14; and Luke 13:3-5). These passages seem to suggest that people (body and soul) will be in a state of utter ruin or complete defeat under the wrath of God.[9] This type of ruin and defeat can be described as destruction, perishing, and being killed, even though the condemned are alive and conscious of their eternal destruction (see chapter 7 for further description of hell as a place of destruction but not annihilation).

HELL AS ETERNAL

Jesus also teaches that hell is eternal. In Matthew 18:7-11 He warns His disciples that those who are in danger of hell should repent before they are cast into the hell of 'eternal fire'. Not only does Jesus state that the fire is eternal; He also says that the punishment of hell will be eternal. To those who are workers of evil, Jesus says, 'Depart from Me, accursed ones, into the eternal fire which has been prepared

---

9   Christopher W. Morgan, 'Biblical Theology: Three Pictures of Hell', in Morgan and Peterson (eds), *Hell Under Fire*, 146.

for the devil and his angels... These will depart into eternal punishment' (Matt. 25:41, 46).

In the Gospel of Mark Jesus adds to the notion of eternality with additional imagery of hell. He says that those who cause Christians to stumble will be cast into hell, 'where their worm does not die, and the fire is not quenched' (Mark 9:38-48). The imagery is simple and yet quite disturbing as one understands the depth of the meaning. Typically, the worm is a creature that feasts on decaying things. Those in hell are in the process of dying but never actually cease to be alive. Thus 'their worm' is feasting on their bodies for eternity, and those in hell will be able to feel the unending pain as the worm feeds upon its host. It seems that Jesus is using this imagery as a way of teaching that every person in hell will be alive and able to feel his or her punishment for eternity, without a moment of respite.

Hell as Banishment

Jesus also describes hell as a place of banishment or separation. Since God is omnipresent, one should not think of this separation as a physical or spiritual separation from an omnipresent God.[10] Rather, it seems best to see hell as a banishment or separation from God's kingdom blessings.[11]

---

10 See Benjamin M. Skaug, 'Hell as Everlasting Punishment', in *SBC LIFE: Journal of the Southern Baptist Convention* (September 2016).

11 Morgan, 'Biblical Theology', 147.

To those who are lawbreakers, Jesus will say on the day of judgment, 'Depart from Me, you who practice lawlessness' (Matt. 7:23; see also 25:30), into the 'place of outer darkness; in that place there will be weeping and gnashing of teeth' (8:12). Jesus again speaks of this aspect of separation as hell: 'Depart from Me, accursed ones, into the eternal fire which has been prepared for the devil and his angels' (25:41).

In what sense is someone spatially separated from God? Can someone be physically and spiritually separated from an omnipresent God? By no means! God is in all places at all times, including hell.[12] So how can those in hell be 'separated' or 'banished' from God?

In the Old Testament, the nation of Israel enjoyed the temple of God and thus was said to be in the kingdom of God or 'in the light'. Through Israel's covenant relationship with God, the nation was in the position to receive blessings from God. Those nations not in right relationship with God were spatially outside the temple grounds and thus said to be 'in the dark' or 'separated from God'. The Bible is not implying that they were outside God's authority or reach (see Psalm 2, where God maintains authority over all peoples everywhere). Rather, they were outside God's covenant blessings and were in the position to receive only God's condemnation and wrath.

---

12   Davies, *An Angry God*, 109.

It is in this light that we must understand how hell is banishment or separation. Those inside of God's kingdom receive the blessings of eternal life. Those in hell are outside of such kingdom blessings and are thus separated and banished from them. But this separation is not an existence away from God or His authority or judgment. Rather, hell is the place where those banished and separated from the kingdom of God will endure the realities of God's wrath without blessing or common grace. Thus separation and banishment mean that the wicked are to be separated from God's blessings, but most definitely not His wrath.

When Jesus says of those who do not accept Him as the Son of God that they will be 'thrown into the outer darkness; in that place there will be weeping and gnashing of teeth' (Matt. 22:13), He is saying that those in hell will not receive any of God's kingdom blessings but will receive only His wrath.

JESUS: THE JUDGE OVER HELL

Since Jesus Christ is God the Son and is omnipresent in His divinity, we understand that Jesus is present in hell. The question is, what is Jesus doing in hell? Jesus actually makes the astounding claim that He will be the Judge over hell.[13]

First, Jesus perceives that all who do not accept Him as the God-sent Messiah will suffer the judgment and

---

13 Wellum, *God the Son Incarnate*, 161.

punishment of hell. This truth is seen clearly in John 3:36: 'He who believes in the Son has eternal life; but he who does not obey the Son will not see life, but the wrath of God abides on him.'

In Luke, Jesus says that those who reject Him likewise reject the Father who sent Him: 'The one who listens to you listens to Me, and the one who rejects you rejects Me; and he who rejects Me rejects the One who sent Me' and will suffer great judgment (Luke 10:13-16). Jesus also says, 'Everyone who confesses Me before men, the Son of Man will confess him also before the angels of God; but he who denies Me before men will be denied before the angels of God' (Luke 12:8-9).

Second, Jesus claims that He is the One who is the Lord over the judgment: 'Just as the Father raised the dead and gives them life, even so the Son also gives life to whom He wishes. For not even the Father judges anyone, but He has given all judgment to the Son, so that all will honor the Son even as they honor the Father' (John 5:21-23). This passage means that God the Father has given all judgment over to God the Son to carry out. Since the Son will carry out the perfect will of God the Father at all times, Jesus will accomplish the Father's will and desires in judgment.

Furthermore, the loving Jesus is just in carrying out the Father's judgment: 'I can do nothing on My own initiative. As I hear, I judge; and My judgment is just, because I do not seek My own will, but the will of Him who sent Me' (John 5:30). In other words, since the judgment of God the Father will be perfect, so too will be that of the Son, as He judges in exact accordance to the will of the Father. Both Father and Son are divine and are therefore omniscient and omnipresent. Thus, just as the Father knows all sins committed against Him throughout human history in all places, so too does the Son. And the Son will rightly and justly condemn all unrepentant sinners to hell on the day of judgment.

Therefore, we can draw two conclusions. First, we can conclude that Jesus is the One who determines who will be condemned to hell. Second, we can conclude that the only basis for not being sentenced to hell is belief in Jesus as the Messiah (see chapter 5). Thus we should assume that Jesus is the Judge over both heaven and hell. As God the Son, His perfect knowledge allows Jesus to exercise perfect universal justice without error. Every single person whom the Son of God sentences to hell will be there rightly and fairly.

SUMMARY OF JESUS ON HELL

Jesus' love did not lead Him to reject hell or to minimize it. Instead, His love required Him to teach that hell is real. More specifically, Jesus taught:

• Hell is the place of divine punishment where God dispenses universal justice.

- The punishment will be dispensed by God and is 'God's wrath'.
- All unrepentant sinners will be rightly sentenced to hell by Jesus, who is the Judge over hell.
- The people in hell will be fully conscious and will feel the agony of God's wrath.
- The punishment in hell is eternal.
- Those in hell are banished and separated from God's kingdom blessings and will know only God's eternal wrath.
- Those in hell will be in the process of destruction and in total ruin, but never annihilated.

If Jesus is right about hell, then it is absolutely the last place anyone would want to be.

Before we turn to the question of avoiding hell, we will first look at the disciples and followers of Jesus to ensure that they understood hell in a similar way as the Creator of hell did. In the next chapter we will ask, what did the apostles teach about hell?

4

What Did the Loving Apostles Teach about Hell?

WHO ARE THE APOSTLES?

W hen it comes to military mission effectiveness, various countries rely on their special forces. These forces receive unparalleled training so that they can be called 'the best of the best'. In the United States of America, one of those great special forces is the Navy SEAL program. Not only are these soldiers selected from the best that the U.S. Navy can offer, but they arrive at their six-month training course with basic military training already under their belts. However, when they arrive at BUD/S (Basic Underwater Demolition/SEAL) training, they are pushed beyond their limits week after week so that their bodies go further than they ever imagined. They are trained in conditioning, combat, stealth tactics, dive tactics, weaponry, and demolitions at levels most of us could not imagine.

Each Navy SEAL is also trained in the same tactics as were their predecessors so that they can be plugged into other functioning teams without tremendous variance. In other words, the heart of the Navy SEAL program is the ability to 'plug and play' these elite soldiers into and out of SEAL teams without compromising the team as a whole.

In the previous chapter, we looked at who Jesus claimed to be according to the Bible and what He taught about hell. What we did not cover was the group of men who followed Him as disciples in training. Most of these twelve men spent over two full years with Jesus. During that time He trained them in ethics, theology, prayer, morality, law, wisdom, and love for others. In short, He taught them everything they would need in order to carry out their ministry for Jesus after He departed. This special group of disciples is collectively referred to as the apostles.

APOSTLES: SPECIAL FOLLOWERS OF JESUS

The apostles were those special followers of Jesus who learned from Him and were appointed by Him to teach and proclaim that He was the Messiah of God. But their teachings were not their own. Rather, they taught the same teachings as their Master, Jesus. Because they learned from Jesus and taught His philosophies, we should expect their views on hell to be quite similar to His. Moreover, we should expect their ethics and morality to be modeled after Jesus as well.

APOSTLES: FOLLOWERS OF JESUS ON LOVE

The apostles were called to be an extension of Jesus' ministry. Because Jesus was one of the most loving people who ever lived, so too should His apostles be known for their love. This loving group was sacrificial and loving on behalf of the suffering and the marginalized. If *they* teach about hell, their love and integrity in personal relationships might encourage us to listen, even if contemporary Christians often disappoint us.

The apostle Paul, also chosen to be an apostle by [the risen] Jesus, wrote one of the Bible's most important treatments on love. First Corinthians 13 speaks about the excellence of love. There Paul says that those who use their gifts for the church without love are as irritating as 'clanging symbols' (v. 1). He even describes love in such a way that many non-Christians have heard his words on the subject from verses 4-8:

> Love is patient, love is kind and is not jealous; love does not brag and is not arrogant, does not act unbecomingly; it does not seek its own, is not provoked, does not take into account a wrong suffered, does not rejoice in unrighteousness, but rejoices with

the truth; bears all things, believes all things, hopes all things, endures all things. Love never fails.

The author to the letter to the Hebrews also writes about love.[1] He reminds his readers that they must continue to love one another. But this is a love that results in action. Out of love, 'do not neglect to show hospitality to strangers… Remember the prisoners, as though in prison with them, and those who are ill-treated' (Heb. 13:2-3). Not only is this letter filled with important instructions on many subjects, but one of them is love and general concern for groups of people (prisoners and the ill-treated) that are often forgotten.

The apostle James is also known for his love and his insistence that love is best understood through action. James chastises the rich who treat the poor in an unbecoming manner. He even gets after Christians for showing partiality toward the rich and against the poor (James 2:1-13). He also warns his readers about the wickedness of our speech as we tear down others (3:1-6), while insisting that true faith is the care of widows and orphans: 'Pure and undefiled religion in the sight of our God and Father is this: to visit orphans and widows in their distress and to keep oneself unstained by the world' (1:27). In other words, love is not

---

1   While we do not know who wrote the letter of Hebrews, we do know that it has authority from one of the apostles.

merely demonstrated through speech but is also seen in one's actions throughout life.

The apostle Peter writes: 'Above all, keep fervent in your love for one another, because love covers a multitude of sins' (1 Pet. 4:8). Peter is able to write this because he has seen the love of Jesus Christ cover the multitude of his own sins. Peter, as we remember from the Gospel accounts, is the disciple who denied the Lord on three occasions after Jesus was arrested. He denied knowing Jesus and denied associating with Him. And yet, after Jesus was crucified and resurrected from the dead, Jesus showed Peter true forgiveness: '"Simon [Peter], son of John, do you love Me?" He said to Him, "Yes, Lord; You know that I love You." He said to Peter, "Shepherd My sheep"' (John 21:17). As Peter writes to fellow believers who are being persecuted, he can give them the same message of love and forgiveness that he received from Jesus.

The apostle John is called the 'beloved disciple'. In fact, in the Gospel of John he refers to himself as 'the disciple whom Jesus loved' on four occasions (John 13:23; 19:26; 21;7; 21:20). Some have interpreted this phrase as arrogance on John's part. But it is more likely humility. It seems that John does not think himself worthy of the love of Christ and therefore does not use his own name in his letter. John is also the apostle who writes that God is love: 'The one who does not love does not know God, for God is love'

(1 John 4:8). He also writes of God's love for humanity: 'For God so loved the world that He gave His only begotten Son, that whosoever believes in Him shall not perish, but have eternal life' (John 3:16).

These apostles were not hard men who were out to get people. Rather, they were the followers and disciples of the most loving person in the world. The love of Jesus transformed them and, through their efforts, the world.[2] And several of these men have written about love and hell. It might not seem like these two issues go hand in hand, but, from the apostles' perspective, the love of God through Jesus Christ is the only thing that can keep people out of hell. Therefore, the apostles write deeply on the subject of hell so that their readers can see it for what it is and become more convinced of the only means of escape.

APOSTLES: FOLLOWING JESUS ON HELL

Naturally, the apostles' teaching on hell is quite similar to that of Jesus. After all, He was their Master, and they were His disciples. His teaching was to be the content of their teaching as they sought to make other people disciples of Jesus as well (Matt. 28:18-20).

In this chapter, we will see what Paul, the author of Hebrews, James, Peter, Jude, and John believed about hell.

---

2   See William Edgar, *Does Christianity Really Work?*, The Big Ten, ed. James N. Anderson and Greg Welty (Fearn, Ross-shire, UK: Christian Focus), 2016.

We should expect these teachings to overlap significantly with Jesus and with one another.

WHAT DOES PAUL TEACH ABOUT HELL?

HELL AS JUDGMENT

Paul does not use the word 'hell' but teaches on it often with images and concepts such as 'death', 'perish', 'destroy', 'wrath', 'condemnation', 'eternal judgment', and 'judgment'.[3] Therefore we will work through some of his writings and examine his understanding of hell as seen from these concepts.

First, Paul argues that all sinners will be judged by God. In Romans 1:18–2:16 he goes further and affirms that all people everywhere without exception have sinned against God and are condemned as law-breakers. He concludes: 'All have sinned and fall short of the glory of God' (Rom. 3:23; see also Eph. 2:1-10). No mere human has kept the law of God, and therefore no one is immune from God's judgment. Not only will those who are guilty be sentenced to hell, but they will face God's judgment for sinning against the Most Holy God: 'The wages of sin is death' (Rom. 6:23), and 'The sins of some men are quite evident, going before them to judgment' (5:24). God will pour out His wrath against 'all

---

3   See Douglas J. Moo, 'Paul on Hell', in Morgan and Peterson (eds), *Hell Under Fire*, 91-2.

ungodliness and unrighteousness' (1:18), and this wrath will be 'upon them to the utmost' (1 Thess. 2:16).

Second, Paul agrees with Jesus that God's punishment in hell is just: 'After all it is only just for God to repay with affliction those who afflict you' (2 Thess. 1:6).[4] In this passage, Christians have been persecuted for their belief in Jesus Christ as the Messiah. Paul is comforting them by reminding them of God's righteousness. He says that God is just in bringing condemnation against those who persecute His people. In other words, God's punishment of law-breakers is good, just, and right. Put another way, Paul is saying that if God withholds judgment against sinners, then He is being unjust.

Paul teaches that God's repayment of punishment in hell is righteous and just because it is a perfect retribution. He writes: 'We must all appear before the judgment seat of Christ, so that each one may be recompensed for his deeds in the body' (2 Cor. 5:10). All people will be recompensed, or paid back, for their sins. And since God does not operate outside of His nature, we should understand that God's repayment, or recompense, is right and just as He 'deals out retribution to those who do not know God and to those who do not obey the gospel of our Lord Jesus' (2 Thess. 1:8). To conclude, Paul is stating that God will pay back law-

---

4   Robert A. Peterson, 'Systematic Theology: Three Vantage Points', in Morgan and Peterson *Hell Under Fire*, 156.

breakers for their sins against Him, and that repayment is perfectly just.

HELL AS ETERNAL

According to Paul, the punishment that God dispenses in hell will be for an eternal duration.[5] He writes: 'These will pay the penalty of eternal destruction from the Lord's presence and from His glorious strength in that day when He comes to be glorified by His saints and to be admired by all those who have believed' (2 Thess. 1:9-10, HCSB). The penalty of destruction that one pays in hell is eternal. The destruction that law-breakers face in hell will not end after a certain period of time. It will not come to a close. Those who are destroyed in hell are not in fact ultimately destroyed, as in annihilation (see chapter 6). Rather, it will continue on and on without end.

HELL AS DESTRUCTION AND DEATH

Paul uses the description of destruction and death frequently as an image of the eternal punishment of hell (Rom. 6:23; Phil. 1:28). In Romans 9:22 he states that those who face hell are 'vessels of wrath prepared for destruction'. Again, destruction here does not mean cessation from existence but teaches that the people have ceased to be what they were created to be, namely, people who bring God glory

---

5   Moo, 'Paul on Hell', 102.

through right worship.[6] In this sense, their suffering in hell is the acknowledgment of their failure to be what God has created them to be. Thus, much like a sports team is 'utterly destroyed' in a landslide defeat even though the team continues to exist, so too are those in hell destroyed as they come to complete loss and ruin.

In 2 Thessalonians 1:9-10 Paul states that hell is 'eternal destruction from the Lord's presence and from His glorious strength.' This passage teaches that God's wrath is not carried out by a secondary source. Rather, this punishment is by the Lord's very presence and strength and is called eternal destruction. That is, those who are under God's wrath are eternally ruined and destroyed (1 Tim 6:9) but never annihilated. In this way, those who are the 'enemies of the cross of Christ, whose end is destruction' (Phil. 3:19) will come to total loss while remaining fully conscious for eternity.

Hell as accursed from Christ

In Romans 9:3 Paul expresses his fervent desire that his own kinsmen (Israel) would see and believe that Jesus Christ is the Messiah. His desire is such that he basically states that he would gladly suffer God's wrath in hell if the entire nation

---

6   For a thorough treatment on 'destruction' see Moo, 'Paul on Hell', 91-109.

of Israel could be saved.[7] He says: 'I wish that I myself were accursed from [by] Christ for the sake of my brethren, my kinsmen according to the flesh.'

Paul fully understands that being accursed by God results in divine wrath in hell. Moreover, Paul recognizes that Jesus is the person of the Trinity who pours out divine wrath on the ungodly in hell: 'I wish that I myself were accursed from [by] Christ.' Even in this vivid description of hell, Paul shows love as he states that he would gladly take the suffering and pain in hell if it meant that all of his kinsmen would be saved through faith in Jesus Christ.

JESUS AS THE JUDGE OVER HELL

As Paul is addressing those gathered at the Areopagus (a gathering place for speakers in ancient Athens), he states that Jesus is the One to whom the Father has given all judgment. He says: 'Having overlooked the times of ignorance, God is now declaring to men that all people everywhere should repent because He has fixed a day in which He will judge the world in righteousness through a Man [Jesus] whom He has appointed, having furnished proof to all men by raising Him [Jesus] from the dead' (Acts 17:30-31). Elsewhere he refers to 'the day when, according to my gospel, God will judge the secrets of men through Christ Jesus' (Rom. 2:16). Jesus is the 'judge of the living and the dead' and will judge

---

7   Morgan, 'Biblical Theology', 140.

all humanity (2 Tim. 4:1-5). It is the 'judgment seat of Christ' that all humanity must stand before in order to give account (2 Cor. 5:10). Paul's teaching about Jesus as the final Judge appointed by God the Father is consistent with the teachings of Jesus, Peter, and John. Again, in this passage we should see that there is a day in which the entire world will be judged, and that Jesus is the final judge.

Furthermore, when Jesus judges all people, He will do so in full righteousness (Rom. 3:1-19; 2 Tim. 4:6-15). In other words, Jesus, through His divine omniscience, will be able to make right and just judgments for each person. Those whom He allows into heaven will rightly be there. Likewise, those whom He consigns to hell will rightly deserve to be there.

Jesus as the Dispenser of divine wrath in Hell

According to Paul, not only is Jesus the righteous judge over hell, but He is also the One who dispenses God's wrath on sinners for eternity. Paul says that wrath and affliction in hell will be poured out when 'the Lord Jesus will be revealed from heaven with His mighty angels in flaming fire, dealing out retribution to those who do not know God and to those who do not obey the gospel of our Lord Jesus. These will pay the penalty of eternal destruction from the Lord's presence and from His glorious power' (2 Thess. 1:7-9). In other words, Paul knows that God's wrath is poured out by Jesus as the Son of God. Jesus does not sit idly by as the Father pours out divine wrath. Rather, we should understand that all judgment has been given from the Father to the Son. This judgment is not merely the proclamation of who is guilty and who is not but is the entire work of judgment. Jesus as God the Son will declare the guilt of law-breakers, and He will carry out their eternal punishment in wrath (Rom. 9:3).

WHAT DOES THE AUTHOR OF HEBREWS TEACH ABOUT HELL?

HELL AS ETERNAL JUDGMENT

Hell is where God will judge and punish law-breakers. The author of Hebrews is in agreement with the rest of Scripture on this point (and on all of his points). He also agrees that the duration of hell is eternal (Heb. 6:2). Moreover, he states that 'eternal judgment' is one of the elementary and foundational teachings (6:1-2) of the Christian faith.[8] He writes:

> Leaving the elementary teaching about the Christ, let us press on to maturity, not laying again a foundation of repentance from dead works and of faith toward God, of instruction about washing and laying on of hands, and the resurrection of the dead and eternal judgment. And this we will do if God permits. For in the case of those who have once been enlightened and have tasted of the heavenly gift and have been

---

8   Ibid., 140.

> made partakers of the Holy Spirit and have tasted of
> the good word of God and the powers of the age to
> come, and then to have fallen away, it is impossible
> to renew them again to repentance, since they again
> crucify to themselves the Son of God and put Him to
> open shame. (Heb. 6:1-6)

The author of Hebrews is urging beleaguered believers to continue their faith in Jesus, since walking away from Christ will invoke the wrath of God in eternal judgment. He does not expound upon this judgment further, since it is such a rudimentary and accepted teaching. Rather, he spends his time pleading with his audience to maintain their faith so that they will avoid God's punishment in hell.

HELL AS SUFFERING

The punishment in hell will not only be eternal but will also be frightening. Those who are sentenced to hell should expect their punishment to be 'the fury of fire which will consume the adversaries' (Heb. 10:27). The pains of the fires of hell will be all-consuming as well as unrelenting. This fact of 'terrifying expectation of judgment' should serve as a warning to all of us to repent for our crimes against God (10:27), who is a 'consuming fire' (12:29). The author of Hebrews also states that 'it is a terrifying thing to fall into the hands of the living God' (10:31). This statement does not assume that those facing this 'living God' will receive any greater punishment than what is deserved. After all, God is exacting justice for crimes (10:30). Rather, this 'living God' is the God of perfection. His wrath, like all of His other actions, will be perfect. Thus the unrepentant sinner should be terrified in facing this God as an eternal adversary.

WHAT DOES JAMES TEACH ABOUT HELL?

HELL AS JUDGMENT WITHOUT MERCY

James warns transgressors of God's laws that hell will be the place of divine judgment (James 4:11-12). Furthermore, that judgment will be without mercy: 'Judgment will be merciless to the one who has shown no mercy' (2:13). Those who are known for being cruel and unmerciful to God's people should expect God's wrath to be poured out on them without mixture of mercy. In this way, God will pay back, or recompense, the wicked for their crimes.

HELL AS PUNISHMENT

This divine judgment of hell is painful. James describes this future punishment as the 'fires of hell' (3:6). The fire imagery of hell seems to indicate that just as one can feel the heat of a fire, so too can one feel the pain of hell. James also says that those who oppress God's people should expect to 'weep and howl for your miseries which are coming upon you' (5:1).[9] Much like the rest of Scripture states that the pain in hell will result in 'wailing and gnashing of teeth', James teaches

---

9   Ibid.

that hell will be extremely painful as God 'pays back' (2:13) the wicked. James also states that God's wrath in hell is just in that it is punishment for what the law-breaker stores up in this life (5:1-3). Thus, while the punishment is painful, it is no more than the law-breaker has 'stored up'.

HELL AS DESTRUCTION

James also states that hell is destruction and death. He warns that those who chase after the pursuits of life will be destroyed just like a hot summer wind punishes grass and flowers (1:11). This quest for life's follies results in a life of sin against God and will lead to a punishment that is death (1:15; 5:20). All judgment is from God, as He alone is the lawgiver and the One who can save people for heaven or destroy them in hell (4:12).

WHAT DO PETER AND JUDE TEACH ABOUT HELL?

HELL AS PUNISHMENT FOR LAW-BREAKERS

The souls of those who break God's laws are kept 'under punishment for the day of judgment' (2 Pet. 2:9), just as the 'present heavens and earth are being reserved for fire, kept for the day of judgment and destruction of ungodly men' (3:7). That day of judgment is also called the 'Day of the Lord' (2 Pet. 3:10) or the 'judgment of the great day' (Jude 6) and will commence God's punishment of all law-breakers for eternity in hell.

Hell is also understood as the place where God pays back 'the wages', or recompenses those who have done wrong (2 Pet. 2:13).[10] In other words, hell is where God will dispense His perfect wrath as a form of remuneration for sin. There will be no injustice in hell, as law-breakers will receive what they have earned in this life.

HELL IS DESTRUCTION

Peter tends to call the eternal punishment of hell destruction. In fact, this image of hell is the one Peter uses most often. He says that those who turn away from God are bringing swift 'destruction upon themselves' (2 Pet. 2:1, 6, 12) and that those who distort the Scriptures are headed 'to their own destruction' (2 Pet. 3:16).

JESUS AS THE JUDGE OVER HELL

One of the first truths Peter states about hell is the fact that Jesus is Judge over the domain of hell. He describes how God 'ordered us to preach to the people, and solemnly to testify that this is the One who has been appointed by God as Judge of the living and the dead. Of Him all the prophets bear witness that through His name everyone who believes in Him receives the forgiveness of sins' (Acts 10:42-43). In other words, Peter is agreeing with Jesus that the Father has

---

10 Ibid., 141.

given all judgment over to the Son. Thus it is the Son of God, Jesus Christ, who will judge all people.

Hell as Eternal

Jude calls hell's judgment the 'punishment of eternal fire' (Jude 7). Again, we must not pit 'destruction' and 'eternal fire' against one another, as though the biblical writers are in conflict. Rather, the two ideas coincide: hell is the eternal process of dying and being destroyed without ever actually being destroyed. Those in hell are those who have completely destroyed their lives and are judged in hell for eternity for breaking God's laws.

WHAT DOES JOHN TEACH ABOUT HELL?

Hell begins with the Day of Judgment

In the book of Revelation, which John the apostle wrote, John hears one of the angels proclaim that God's day of judgment is about to begin: 'Fear God, and give Him glory, because the hour of His judgment has come; worship Him who made the heaven and the earth and sea and springs of waters' (Rev. 14:7). John is telling his readers of a final day of judgment. This final day will be too late to repent of one's sins against God and find refuge in the Son, Jesus Christ. Once the day of judgment, or the Day of the Lord, arrives, there will not be another opportunity to change the course of one's eternal destination. Thus the book of Revelation warns people that the last day is looming and that they should repent and seek God's means of escape from judgment while there is still time.

Those who are sentenced to the judgments of hell are the nations (Rev. 11:18), those who violate God's laws or the 'cowardly and unbelieving and abominable and murderers and immoral persons and sorcerers and idolaters and all liars[;] their part will be in the lake that burns with fire and brimstone, which is the second death' (Rev. 21:8). Moreover, all people who are not found to be in 'the book of life' are cast into hell (20:15).

JESUS AS THE JUDGE OVER HELL

Just as the rest of the New Testament claims that Jesus is the One who is Judge over heaven and hell, so too does Revelation. In Revelation 1:18 Jesus is described as having the keys to death and Hades. This image affirms that Jesus is the Judge who determines the final outcome of all people. The keys are a symbol of authority and access that Jesus has received from the Father.

HELL AS DEATH

John says that those who have faith in Christ and overcome tribulation will not be 'hurt by the second death' (Rev. 2:11). This image seems to represent the pain of hell, as it is also called the 'lake of fire' (20:14; 21:8). The Devil, the false prophet, the beast (20:10), and all who are not listed in the book of life (20:15) will be thrown into the lake of fire.[11] This lake of fire that is the second death is also described through the painful images of 'the lake that burns with fire and brimstone', into which all law-breakers are cast (Rev. 21:8).

HELL AS DIVINE PUNISHMENT

Once again, hell is described as the just retribution from God (Rev. 6:10). This punishment is described as 'torment' and 'fire' as the Lord pours out His wrath on law-breakers (18:6-8).

Hell is further described as the place where the wicked justly endure 'the great wine press of the wrath of God' (Rev. 14:19; 6:17). This wrath is poured out on law-breakers to the fullest extent possible. Revelation 14:10 describes this wrath as 'the wine of the wrath of God which is mixed in full strength in the cup of His anger.' In other words, God's divine punishment will not have any hint of mercy in it, as hell is the 'full strength' of the omnipotent God's wrath.[12]

---

11   Christopher W. Morgan rightly states that the Bible is clear that the devil is 'thrown' into the lake of fire, meaning that Satan does not rule this domain in any capacity. Rather, he will be thrown into hell for eternity along with the beast, the false prophet, and all of those who are not named in the book of life. See Morgan, 'Biblical Theology', 141.

12   Ibid.

HELL'S PUNISHMENT AS RIGHTEOUS

John describes God's wrath in hell as righteous. Revelation 16:5-7 declares: 'Righteous are You, who are and who were, O Holy One, because You judged these things: for they poured out the blood of the saints and prophets, and You have given them blood to drink. They deserve it. And I heard the altar saying, "Yes, O Lord God, the Almighty, true and righteous are Your judgments."' Again, since it is the perfect, holy, righteous, and loving God who guarantees cosmic justice, all of His actions and judgments are, by definition, good, righteous, and true. His actions in hell will not be exceptions to this truth.

Furthermore, God's actions in hell against the wicked are deemed praiseworthy. Seen from the correct perspective, those in heaven will praise God for dispensing perfect justice against those who have committed egregious crimes against God and His people: 'Rejoice over her,[13] O heaven, and you saints and apostles and prophets, because God has pronounced judgment for you against her' (Rev. 18:20). The population of heaven is not a collection of bloodthirsty people from the Coliseum. Rather, they are those who are cheering and praising God for ensuring that no law-breaker escapes the punishment that he or she deserves: 'Hallelujah! Salvation and glory and power belong to our God. Because

---

13 'Her' in this passage refers to the city of Babylon as representative of those who are against God and His people.

His judgments are true and righteous: for He has judged the great harlot who was corrupting the earth with her immorality, and He has avenged the blood of His bond-servants on her' (19:1-2). God's actions are right, good, true, and even praiseworthy as He dispenses universal justice without error.

JESUS AS THE ONE WHO DISPENSES PUNISHMENT IN HELL

Not only does John show Jesus to be the righteous and just Judge over hell; he also displays Jesus as the One who dispenses divine wrath. As the kings of the earth who have rebelled against God are about to receive their deserved punishment in hell, they cry out to the mountains, 'Fall on us and hide us from the presence of Him who sits on the throne, and from the wrath of the Lamb; for the great day of their wrath has come, and who is able to stand?' (Rev. 6:16-17).[14]

Jesus is the loving man who commands His followers to love their enemies, and He is God the Son who will have all judgment turned over to Him. Part of this judgment is the actual carrying out of divine punishment. Thus the loving

---

14 John uses the term 'lamb' here as a direct reference to Jesus, much like he does in his Gospel. See John the Baptist's saying of Jesus: 'Behold, the Lamb of God that takes away the sin of the world' (John 1:29). It is also clear from the book of Revelation itself that Jesus is the Lamb, as He is the referent in Revelation 5 who has purchased people with His blood and is then worthy of worship (Rev. 5:1-14).

Jesus will pour out the 'wrath of the Lamb' to a precise degree for eternity. His love, while true, will not overrule His justice or holiness.

HELL AS DESTRUCTION

John hears the loud voices in heaven and the elders warning that the reign of Jesus Christ is coming soon. The reign of Jesus includes the rewarding of His faithful people in heaven as well as the pouring out of wrath in hell. That wrath of Jesus will destroy His enemies just as they 'destroyed the earth' (Rev. 11:17-18). Those who are sentenced to hell are said to 'go to destruction' (17:8-11) as they endure God's wrath in hell.

HELL AS ETERNAL

Revelation coincides with the teachings of Jesus as well as the rest of the Bible as it describes hell as the place of eternal punishment. Revelation 14:11 uses graphic language to show the eternal nature of those who are being punished in hell: 'The smoke of their torment goes up forever and ever; they have no rest day and night.' 'Smoke of their torment' seems to show the wrath of God as poured out in 'full mixture', while 'no rest day and night' seems to reference the eternality of punishment.

Moreover, Revelation describes hell as the place where the Devil, the beast, the false prophet, law-breakers, and those not found in the book of life are cast and where 'they will be tormented day and night forever and ever' (20:10, 13, 15; 21:8). Once God's wrath begins in hell, it continues for eternity.

HELL CONTINUES TO EXIST AFTER THE FINAL JUDGMENT

It is also noteworthy that John describes hell as part of the landscape of the new creation. In his amazing description of the new heavens and the new earth (Rev. 21:1-8), John also describes the lake of fire and those who are added to Satan's, the beast's, and the false prophet's destination:

> He who overcomes will inherit these things, and I will be his God and he will be My Son. But for the cowardly and unbelieving and abominable and murderers and immoral persons and sorcerers and idolaters and all liars, their part will be in the lake that burns with fire and brimstone, which is the second death.

The new creation does not contain heaven without hell. It contains both heaven and hell as God demonstrates His perfect love (heaven) and justice (hell) for eternity.

SUMMARY OF HELL ACCORDING TO THE APOSTLES

It should not surprise us that the apostles teach what Jesus taught. They were His followers and disseminated His teachings on all subjects, including love, charity, hope, help of the poor, support for the helpless, and hell. While each loving apostle might emphasize one picture of hell more than the others do, we can see that the overall teaching is consistent throughout the New Testament:

- Hell is punishment for breaking God's laws.
- Hell is extremely painful.
- Hell is suffering.
- Hell is destruction.
- Hell is deserved.
- The punishment in hell is the precise punishment required for God to maintain His holiness and righteousness.
- God's wrath in hell is just recompense and retribution of crimes committed against God.
- Jesus is the One who dispenses God's wrath in hell.
- Hell is the second death.
- Hell is eternal conscious punishment.

The reality of hell is overwhelming. At this point some readers might be tempted to put down this book out of discouragement or even disgust. But I want to encourage you to continue reading, because in the next chapter we will see the absolute love of God shine forth in one ray of hope for all people. God has not left us in our sins and trespasses. He has provided a means of escape. But that means of escape, as we will see in chapter 5, requires faith.

5

How Can Hell Be Avoided?

In 1994 Columbia Pictures released their rendition of Stephen King's 1982 novella, *Rita Hayworth and Shawshank Redemption*. This Frank Darabont directed movie was titled *The Shawshank Redemption* and starred Tim Robbins as Andy Dufresne and Morgan Freeman as Ellis 'Red' Redding. It was nominated for seven Academy Awards and received two Golden Globe awards. The story is written around Andy's wrongful imprisonment and eventual escape from Shawshank State Penitentiary.

Most of us cringe at the thought of facing two decades in a horrific penitentiary for a crime we did not commit. Spending that much time being punished for something we did not do would be torment beyond comprehension. I think one of the reasons this movie is so compelling is because we can relate to Andy's desire for freedom. Most of us, if wrongfully imprisoned, might do anything in the world to get ourselves out—to be free once again. It speaks to us about the lengths to which one man might go in order to escape his living hell in prison.

Andy spent 16.9 years of his prison sentence tunneling through a 10-foot-thick wall. If the math is right, then he tunneled about 1/64 of an inch every day for 16.9 years. Then, when the timing was right, he lowered himself down onto the main sewer pipe and created a hole large enough to fit through. Then he crawled through 500 yards of human waste before he found freedom. That is just shy of a third of a mile. If you have seen the movie, you can probably still see with your mind's eye Andy Dufresne crawling out of the sewer pipe and then standing in the rain with his arms raised in victory as he has obtained his freedom. It is a moving moment and one that sticks with those who have seen the film.

The question remains: if we were in that position, would we not do whatever it took in order to obtain our freedom?

Well, if the Bible is right, and God's nature demands that He punish all law-breakers in hell—and all of us are certainly law-breakers—then would we be willing to take any method of escape from God's eternal wrath? Most of us, if convinced that hell was real, would do whatever it took in order to avoid it. What if there were only one way out of hell: would we take it? If we knew that God ordained one particular means of escape from hell, would we accept His offer? I think that most people, if convinced of the horrors of hell, would do whatever it took to escape it.

The question now moves to God: will His nature allow Him to create a means of escaping hell? The answer is yes. But this means of escape is by God's own design and consistent with His complete character. In other words, He cannot simply declare, 'I forgive sins!' His perfect holy nature necessitates that law-breaking be met with a just punishment. Recall from chapter 2 that God's holy nature requires that only those who are sinless and obedient to all of His laws can be allowed to escape hell and enter heaven. Thus the means of escape that God creates is one whereby sins can be forgiven but the penalties of death and wrath are still poured out.

But having our sins and law-breaking taken away from us in a just manner is not enough for us to enter God's heaven. In other words, being sinless is only half of the necessary requirements to enter God's heaven. We must also earn righteousness from our perfect obedience to God's law. We can better understand this truth as we remember Adam and Eve in the garden of Eden. Before the fall, they were both sinless but lacked righteousness through obedience. This condition kept them from being allowed in heaven. Thus the testing in the garden of Eden was an opportunity for Adam to earn righteousness through obedience. Instead of earning righteousness, however, Adam disobeyed God's law through sin and was then brought to face God's wrath.

Therefore, we must understand that the only means of escape from hell that allows anyone into heaven must be through both perfect obedience and perfect sinlessness. Our problem arises from the fact that our fallen nature prevents us from obeying God and causes us to sin instead. Thus, we lack the righteousness we are supposed to have while bearing the sinfulness we are supposed to avoid. If we are left in this condition, we will always be in the position of deserving God's wrath. Since we cannot save ourselves, we have to look elsewhere for any hope of salvation!

GOD'S LOVE CREATES A WAY OF SALVATION

First, let us clear the air about a very important fact: God did not have to create this universe, and He certainly did not have to create you or me. But He did create us! He gave us life, and we have good things that have all come from Him. We have all had good days where we are happy and surrounded by people we love. These things are not owed to us as members of the human race. Rather, these are from God's benevolent grace. The fact that we live and breathe is God's common grace that He gives to all people indiscriminately, but not to all equally. When I say that it is not equal, I mean that not all people live to the same age or receive the same blessings in this life.

Second, since our mere existence is by God's grace and mercy, then any means or opportunity to be saved from hell and enter into God's heaven would be additional divine grace. In other words, we certainly do not deserve any opportunity to be saved. God does not owe anyone an opportunity to be saved from His just judgment. So the fact that God creates a means by which people can be saved from His eternal wrath is an incredible demonstration of His amazing love and grace.

In this chapter, we will consider God's plan of salvation as our sole means of escape from hell.

CAN GOD JUST CHOOSE TO FORGIVE SINS?

At one point or another, many people have asked themselves this question: 'If we have all sinned against God, then why can He not just choose to forgive us? Why does there have to be any more to it than that?' This is a good question that returns us to God's nature and holiness.

God is holy. To be holy means to be completely devoid of sin. Everything that God does is right and upright. He has not sinned, nor will He ever sin, as any thought or action of sin would be contrary to His nature. He will always act in a manner that is righteous and just.

Since God is perfectly holy and just, He cannot allow law-breaking to go unpunished. It is not in His nature to allow a crime to go unpunished. Much like a courtroom judge should not allow the laws of the land to be broken without just punishment, so too God will uphold the laws He has placed on the universe. Where there is infraction, God will necessarily bring about a just punishment.

The Bible is clear about the just and necessary punishment for any and all law-breaking: 'The wages of sin is death' (Rom. 6:23). This verse indicates not that the wages of a *lifetime* of sin is death but rather that the wages of *any* sin is death. As we discussed in chapters 3–4, death is one of the images for God's wrath being poured out on the wicked in hell. Thus, when the Bible states that 'all have sinned and fall short of the glory of God' (Rom. 3:23), it is saying that all people everywhere are law-breakers and under the just punishment of death. In other words, when someone violates God's law, then his life is, at that moment, forfeit. In the just actions of the Most Holy God, the Lord will carry out the correct punishment for the crime. Since He is righteous, we should never expect God to bypass this punishment, because that would be a universal injustice.

When we ask God to 'simply forgive sin', we are really asking Him to be unjust! We are asking the very One who defines justice and righteousness to allow crime to go unpunished. Deep down, we know that He cannot allow an injustice, and we know that He will uphold righteousness. To fail in these areas would be to violate His own nature.

In light of these truths, we can come to know how loving God is. Even though God does not *have* to create a means of forgiveness, He *has*! The sovereign God who will maintain His righteousness in regard to crime and punishment has created one way of escape from His wrath. He has created a way in which a completely guilty person can not only receive forgiveness of his or her sins but also be credited with perfect obedience in regard to God's laws. In other words, God has created one way in which we, as guilty people, can be declared both righteous (as if we had obeyed God's laws in every area at all times) and forgiven of all sins (as if we had not broken God's laws at any time). He accomplishes this amazing means of escape while upholding and maintaining righteousness and justice in regard to His laws and nature. What is this means of escape? In the following sections, we will flesh out (briefly) how God can justly declare some people as forgiven and righteous so that they can avoid hell.

GOD'S LOVE CREATES A PRACTICE OF SUBSTITUTION

From the moment that Adam failed to uphold the law and thus cast all humanity into a state of sin, God has been quick to proclaim that He will create a legitimate way out of hell. In Genesis 3:15, God gives the first proclamation of that 'good news'. In essence, He says that He will accomplish this means of escape on behalf of people. But He does not come right out and state His entire plan all at once. Rather,

He allows His plan to unfold more and more as history continues. In other words, the further in human history one is, the more information that person might have. I say 'might have' because God has never promised that all people everywhere will receive God's rescue plan or that all people will have equal opportunities to be part of it.

In order to prepare His people for His full rescue plan, God introduced the practice of substitution. Substitution means that something 'clean' can be substituted for something guilty. As long as the clean thing pays the payment of death on behalf of the guilty thing, the guilty thing that should have died can escape the penalty of death and be allowed to live.

First, the clean thing is an animal that is free from disease and is a perfect specimen of that animal. If the animal is a lamb, the lamb must be a good and right representation of what a lamb must be. It cannot be a ratty old thing obviously on its last legs. Rather, it must be a healthy lamb without spot or blemish. This lamb's identification as clean allows it to represent the righteousness we should have. Since the animal is spotless and without blemish, the animal's life is not forfeit as the just punishment of God for law-breaking. Thus this clean thing represents the notion of innocence and righteousness.

Second, the guilty person is allowed to offer a clean sacrifice in his or her place. In this sacrifice, God allows a two-way transfer to take place. First, the guilty person transfers (or imputes) his or her sin to the clean thing. Second, the clean thing transfers (or imputes) its righteousness to the guilty person. At this moment, the guilty person is now innocent of previous sins committed, as those sins have been transferred to the clean thing. The thing that was previously called clean now stands guilty because of the sins it has assumed. Since the thing that was previously clean is now guilty, it must die as a just punishment for sin. It now stands condemned.

This aspect of substitution stands behind the entire sacrificial system of the Old Testament. These substitutionary sacrifices are in line with God's arrangement that allows a guilty person to continue living since a clean thing has taken its punishment for sin.

GOD'S LOVE DEMONSTRATED IN THE PASSOVER EVENT

This substitutionary system is seen most vividly in the event called the Passover. In Exodus 11-12 we see that all of the lives of the firstborn males are forfeit (presumably for their sins against God). He will arrive on the scene and execute divine wrath on all who lack both sinlessness and righteousness. In light of the threat of divine wrath, the nation of Israel executes what it knows to be the only means by which the guilty persons can escape death and be given life.

The families of Israel each select a lamb without spot or blemish as the clean thing to take the place of the guilty

(Exod. 12:5). They are required to kill the lamb and take its blood and paint it on the doorposts of their homes. This blood is proof that a life has already been taken on behalf of the sinful firstborn. Furthermore, the people inside the home have to eat the flesh of the lamb. The flesh of the clean animal represents righteousness being transferred from the clean animal to the individual. In this way, the necessary death for sin has been paid by the lamb and the son remaining alive has a sense of both forgiveness of sins and also righteousness from the clean animal.

As God visits the land in order to bring divine justice, He graciously passes over every home at which He sees the blood of the substitutionary animal painted on the doorposts, since justice has already been accomplished (Exod. 12:12-13). In this manner, God maintains His justice and allows a gracious system of forgiveness.

THE TEMPORARY NATURE OF THE SACRIFICIAL SYSTEM: HEBREWS 10:1-4

While this system teaches the idea of substitution, the nature of animal sacrifices was a provisional teaching method that would disappear once the full and final reality arrived. Hebrews 10:1 says that this system was merely a 'shadow of the good things to come and not the very form' of the reality to come. It was a shadow because the Bible says that the blood of bulls and goats (all of the sacrificial animals are assumed here) could never actually be effective enough to forgive sin (Heb. 10:4). In and of themselves, these sacrifices were not sufficient to make the guilty person perfect in the sight of God (10:1)!

If the animal's blood were adequate to forgive sins, the sacrificial system would not have required repetition. But the guilty people had to continue to repeat this process yearly. And the people themselves understood that this system needed a final fulfillment, since the repetitious nature of the sacrifices was proof that their forgiveness and righteousness were never in *these* animals. Rather, they conducted these sacrifices in faith, looking forward to the day in which God's ultimate plan of substitution would come to fruition.

GOD'S LOVE IS FULFILLED IN JESUS CHRIST

The Bible says that when 'the fullness of time came God sent forth His Son, born of a woman, born under the Law, so that He might redeem those who were under the Law, that we might receive the adoption as sons' (Gal. 4:4-5). The 'fullness of time' means that God's final solution of perfect forgiveness and loving righteousness arrived at the apex of human history. No other time would have been quite as perfect as this moment for Jesus to be born of a woman.

As we discovered in chapter 3, Jesus is the eternal God the Son and is fully divine. In His divine nature He does not have a moment of birth, since He is eternal. This passage from Galatians is highlighting His human nature, which He adds to His divine nature at the event of the incarnation. In His human nature, He is fully human but without sin or a fallen-sin nature. This miraculous feat is accomplished through the virgin birth: 'The Child who has been conceived in her [Mary] is of the Holy Spirit' (Matt. 1:20).

Jesus as the perfect Law-Keeper

In His earthly life, Jesus is perfectly obedient to God's law. In every capacity, He carries out the will of God and obeys the law without hint of disobedience. Jesus says: 'My food is to do the will of Him who sent Me and to accomplish His work' (John 4:34), and 'I can do nothing on My own initiative. As I hear, I judge, and My judgment is just because I do not seek My own will, but the will of Him who sent Me' (5:30). Jesus does not have His own agenda apart from the Father's. Rather, He perfectly accomplishes that which the Father sends Him to carry out. And He carries it out in a manner which is in line with God's laws: 'Do not think that I have come to abolish the Law or the prophets; I have not come to abolish them but to fulfill them. For I say to you, until heaven and earth pass away, not an iota or a dot will pass away from the Law until all is accomplished' (Matt. 5:17-18, ESV).

Since Jesus keeps God's law perfectly, He earns righteousness through His obedience! Because He is sinless and has righteousness, He is the only One who does not have to fear the wrath of God for law-breaking. He could have kept this righteousness to Himself, but then this would not be the greatest love story ever told. You see, Jesus accomplishes perfection so that He can give it to those who believe and have faith in Him.

JESUS AS THE PERFECT SUBSTITUTE

Since Jesus is without spot or blemish, He is able to become a perfect substitute for His people as He fulfills the Old Testament sacrificial system. Through the plan of God, Jesus transfers (or imputes) His righteousness to His people. All of those who believe in Jesus and have faith in Him receive the righteousness that He has earned through flawless obedience. In Philippians 3:8-9 Paul says that he considers this truth to be worth all of life's struggles:

> I count all things to be loss in view of the surpassing value of knowing Christ Jesus my Lord, for whom I have suffered the loss of all things, and count them but rubbish so that I may gain Christ and may be found in Him, not having a righteousness of my own derived from the Law, but that which is through faith in Christ, the righteousness which comes from God on the basis of faith.

Not only does Jesus provide righteousness for His people, but He also accomplishes the forgiveness of their sins. Just as the sins of the guilty person are transferred to the clean thing in the Old Testament system, so too were all of the sins of God's people transferred to Jesus Christ. All of the sins from God's people were heaped onto Jesus so that He could pay the price of death for those people. He faced the full wrath of God and paid the just punishment for law-breaking that the people of God should have paid for themselves!

Through the substitutionary work of Jesus, those who have faith in Him have their sins forgiven and cannot be counted as law-breakers ever again. In contrast to the animals from the Old Testament, whose sacrifices had to be repeated over and over again, Jesus offered Himself as a sacrifice for sin once and for all and accomplishes that which the clean animals could not. His substitution is so effective that it perfectly cleanses His people from their sins—they can never have those sins counted against them (Heb. 10:10-12).

When does Jesus become our Substitute?

The Bible tells us when and where Jesus becomes the perfect substitute for the people of God. It was at the crucifixion of Jesus, or what many call 'Good Friday'. When Jesus was crucified on the cross, He carried out what is called the 'great exchange'.[1] The sins of the people of God were placed upon Him, and His righteousness was imputed to His people. On

---

1   I learned this concept from Jerry Bridges; see Jerry Bridges and Bob Bevington, *The Great Exchange: My Sins for His Righteousness* (Wheaton, IL: Crossway, 2007).

the cross, the full wrath of God was placed upon the person of Christ, and He died the necessary death that is our penalty to bear. This substitutionary death was strikingly foretold in the Old Testament prophecy of Isaiah 53:

> Surely our griefs He Himself bore, and our sorrows He carried; yet we ourselves esteemed Him stricken, smitten of God, and afflicted. But He was pierced through for our transgressions, He was crushed for our iniquities; the chastening for our well-being fell upon Him, and by His scourging we are healed… But the Lord was pleased to crush Him, putting Him to grief; if He would render Himself as a guilt offering.

Not only does God show His grace and mercy in giving this means of escape, but He also demonstrates that He is still just, as God is both 'just and the justifier' (Rom. 3:26). Since Jesus took the wrath of God on behalf of the people of God, God can forgive their sins and accept them as righteous without diminishing His justice in any capacity. In other words, God has maintained His universal justice and cannot be charged with being unjust.

Jesus' death on the cross is not the end of the story. In fact, the crucifixion of Jesus is meaningless apart from His victory over sin and death through His resurrection from the dead. It is His resurrection, or what many call 'Easter', that gives power and hope to those who place their faith in Him. The Bible says that, after Jesus died His substitutionary death,

He was raised from the dead on the third day: 'He is not here [in the tomb], for He has risen, just as He said. Come, see the place where He was lying. Go quickly and tell His disciples that He has risen from the dead' (Matt. 28:6-7). Those who place their faith in Jesus do not place their trust in a dead sacrifice. Rather, they believe that Jesus died on the cross for them and defeated death through His resurrection from the dead. In other words, believers place their faith and trust in a risen and living Lord who died for them but who also conquered sin and death through His resurrection.

THOSE IN JESUS CHRIST BY FAITH CANNOT BE CONDEMNED TO HELL

The transgressions of the people of God have been placed upon Jesus, and He bore the resultant shame, chastening, and affliction from God. Those sins and the punishment that come with them are paid in full! Romans 8:1 joyfully reads: 'Therefore, there is now no condemnation for those who are in Christ Jesus.' For those who are united to Jesus Christ through faith, God will not condemn them, since their sins have been paid through Jesus' work on the cross.

Since God will not condemn those who believe in Jesus Christ, He will not sentence them to hell, either. On the day of judgment, God will count all those who believe in Jesus as perfectly righteous and will pass over them in judgment. Instead of eternal death in hell, they will be given eternal life in heaven. John 3:16 clearly states: 'God so loved the world that He gave His only begotten Son, so that whoever believes in Him, will not perish, but have everlasting life.' They will not enter that place of eternal destruction, since hell is the place for those who remain condemned in their own sins. Those who have faith in Christ cannot be condemned nor sentenced to eternal death. Rather, by God's grace, they have the right to enter God's heaven and are given eternal life.

God's love is what has brought about this amazing opportunity of escape from hell. It is the love of Jesus as the Son of God who has willingly accepted the role of substitutionary sin-bearer for the people of God. In other words, the single greatest display of true and authentic love in the history of the world is captured in that moment when Jesus took the wrath of God for His people.

HELL REMAINS FOR THOSE WHO DO NOT BELIEVE IN JESUS CHRIST

This amazing escape is the only means by which any human being can escape God's wrath in hell. There are no other ways by which anyone can evade God's universal judgment.

- Jesus said to him: 'I am the way, and the truth, and the life; no one comes to the Father but through me.' (John 14:6)
- '[Jesus] is the stone which was rejected by you, the builders, but which became the chief cornerstone. And

there is salvation in no one else; for there is no other name under heaven that has been given among men by which we must be saved.' (Acts 4:11-12)

Jesus makes this point very clear. There are no other options. There are no other religions that lead to a just escape from hell. There are no other possibilities that allow someone to evade God's judgment. The substitutionary work of Jesus on the cross and His resurrection from the dead are the only means of hope that anyone can have.

Jesus also states: 'He who believes in the Son has eternal life; but he who does not obey the Son will not see life, but the wrath of God abides on him' (John 3:36). In other words, the work of Jesus Christ can be applied only to those who are His by faith. If you are reading this chapter and do not have faith in Jesus, you need to understand that the Bible says that you will face God on the day of final judgment. When that day arrives, you will know, beyond a shadow of a doubt, that you are guilty of breaking God's laws. As a law-breaker, you will face God's just punishment for your sins against Him. You will be sentenced and cast into hell, where you will face God's wrath for eternity. In this act God's righteousness, love, holiness, goodness, and justice will remain intact.

My hope and desire for you is that you will not stand and face God in your own works or efforts. My hope is that you will turn your life over to Jesus Christ. The Bible is clear about those who turn to Him and place their trust, faith, and lives in Him: 'The wages of sin is death, but the free gift of God is eternal life in Christ Jesus our Lord' (Rom. 6:23); and 'If you confess with your mouth that Jesus is Lord and believe with your heart that God raised Him from the dead, you will be saved. For with the heart one believes and is justified, and with the mouth one confesses and is saved' (10:9-10). If you give your life to Jesus Christ, you cannot and will not be condemned to hell (8:1-4). This is God's good news.[2]

In the final two chapters, we will briefly examine two false understandings in regard to hell. In chapter 6 we will look at the false understanding of annihilationism. In chapter 7 we will look at the false understanding of universalism.

---

2 Some helpful resources on the work of Jesus Christ are: Jerry Bridges and Bob Bevington, *The Great Exchange: My Sins for His Righteousness* (Wheaton: Crossway, 2007); Bruce Demarest, *The Cross and Salvation: The Doctrine of Salvation* (Wheaton: Crossway, 1997); Greg Gilbert, *What is the Gospel?* (Wheaton: Crossway, 2010); Robert Letham, *The Work of Christ* (Downers Grove: InterVarsity Press, 1993); R.C. Sproul, *The Work of Christ: What the Events of Jesus Mean for You* (Colorado Springs: David C. Cook, 2012); and John R. Stott, *The Cross of Christ* (Downers Grove: InterVarsity Press, 1986).

6

Is Hell Eternal?

We have seen that hell is described using several images throughout the Bible. All of these images, or what Christopher Morgan calls 'pictures', of hell must be seen together in harmony with one another, lest we end up in theological error.[1]

In recent times, the eternality of hell has come under attack by some who have focused the bulk of their attention on the picture of hell as destruction, banishment, and death (without working together with the other pictures) in order to arrive at a limited divine punishment that ends in annihilation. In this chapter, we will work through what this theory (called *annihilationism*) is, a brief history of the theory, and how the proponents of annihilationism tend to

---

1   Morgan, 'Biblical Theology', 150.

arrive at their conclusions. We will then see if this theory is in line with the Bible's full-orbed description of hell.

WHAT IS ANNIHILATIONISM?

Annihilationism is the theory that those who are condemned to hell will face God's wrath for a limited duration of time before being annihilated to the point of non-existence.[2] This position does seek to uphold the notion of God's wrath being poured out on unrepentant law-breakers. However, those who hold this view maintain that God's wrath should not be eternal in duration. Rather, they believe there will be a moment at which the person will pass into the state of non-being.

A branch of annihilationism called *conditionalism* (or *conditional immortality*) holds to the ultimate annihilation of those condemned to hell, because conditionalists believe that the human soul is not immortal.[3] They maintain that only those who are allowed in heaven due to their faith in Jesus Christ are resurrected and given immortality by God

---

2   There are some in this camp who also maintain that God's punishment is eternal but that the unrighteous are annihilated and therefore cannot consciously feel the punishment after annihilation.

3   Some of the more conservative annihilationists prefer the term *conditionalists* as a way to clarify the notion that they do not hold to an immortal soul. See D. A. Carson, 'On Banishing the Lake of Fire', in D. A. Carson, *The Gagging of God: Christianity Confronts Pluralism* (Grand Rapids, MI: Zondervan, 1996), 516.

so that they can enjoy God's glorious presence for eternity. This immortality is in both body and soul.

Conditionalists do not believe that God grants this same immortality to those designated for hell. While those sentenced to hell are given resurrected bodies for the final judgment, they are not granted immortality in either body or soul. Since they are not granted immortality from God, when they face an undefined period of God's wrath they will be ultimately and finally annihilated and thus cease to exist.[4] Since conditionalism is a branch of annihilationism, we will continue to refer to conditionalists as annihilationists.

WHERE DOES ANNIHILATIONISM COME FROM?

Historically speaking, annihilationism has its roots (somewhat) in the early writing of fourth-century Christian apologist Arnobius of Sicca and his criticism of Plato's belief in the immortality of the human soul. Arnobius argued that the human soul cannot be immortal by nature and that the soul is unable to endure the severity of God's wrath. Therefore, since that soul is not immortal, the human soul in hell will be ultimately annihilated.

While there are a few scattered thinkers who embraced annihilationism before the twentieth century, the vast majority of annihilationist efforts have appeared since

---

4   John W. Wenham, *The Goodness of God* (Downers Grove, IL: InterVarsity Press, 1974), 34-35.

1961, with the most noteworthy works coming from John Wenham, Edward Fudge, Clark Pinnock, John Stott, David Powys, and the Alliance Commission on Unity and Truth among Evangelicals (ACUTE).[5]

HOW DO ANNIHILATIONISTS ARRIVE AT THEIR POSITION?

While there are various camps within annihilationism, it seems as though the disagreement with the historic position stems from three areas: 1) What John Stott calls an 'emotional' recoiling from the idea of hell as eternal conscious punishment, as it seems contrary to God's love and justice; 2) specific language used in the Bible that might suggest annihilation; and 3) a philosophical appeal to a mortal soul.

THE 'EMOTIONAL'[6] AND LOVE OBJECTION

Obviously, there is a real emotional difficulty that many have with the eternal nature and duration of hell. Some annihilationists find themselves asking what purpose an

---

5   For a brief history of annihilationism and conditionalism since 1961 see Christopher W. Morgan, 'Annihilationism: Will the Unsaved Be Punished Forever?' in *Hell Under Fire*, ed. Christopher W. Morgan and Robert A. Peterson (Grand Rapids, MI: Zondervan, 2004), 197-200.

6   This category is taken from Stott's own comments (hence the quotes) and is not used here in any way to be unfair. Rather, it is a real category raised by annihilationists and seems to be the starting point of their position. Thus it deserves a response. David L. Edwards and John Stott, *Evangelical Essentials: A Liberal-Evangelical Dialogue* (Downers Grove, IL: InterVarsity Press, 1988), 314-15.

eternal divine wrath serves. In fact, the Alliance Commission on Unity and Truth Among Evangelicals (ACUTE) noted that this emotional objection seems to be the starting point for those who reject the historical position on hell.[7] John Stott says: 'Emotionally, I find the concept [of eternal punishment] intolerable and do not understand how people can live with it without either cauterizing their feelings or cracking under the strain. But our emotions are a fluctuating, unreliable guide to truth and must not be exalted to the place of supreme authority in determining it.'[8]

Another noted annihilationist scholar, Clark Pinnock, says that the eternal nature of hell is one of the primary reasons to reject the historical position and support conditionalism instead: 'Obviously, I am rejecting the traditional view of hell in part out of a sense of moral and theological revulsion to it. The idea that a conscious creature should have to undergo physical and mental torture through unending time is profoundly disturbing.'[9] He also states that an eternality of divine wrath would be an eternal 'torture chamber' that brings about 'awful moral implications' and is

---

7   *The Nature of Hell: A Report by the Evangelical Alliance Commission on Unity and Truth Among Evangelicals* (Carlisle, UK: ACUTE/ Paternoster, 2000), 102.

8   Stott, *Evangelical Essentials*, 314-15.

9   Clark H. Pinnock, 'The Conditional View', *Four Views on Hell* (Grand Rapids, MI: Zondervan, 1999), 164.

'detrimental to the character of God'.[10] Altogether, Pinnock says that the historical view of hell as eternal punishment is a 'sadistic horror'.[11]

In these statements we can see a strong emotional objection to a loving God who punishes the unrighteous for an eternity. In other words, such scholars have a view of God's love that is incompatible with *eternal* punishment. While they do not argue against God's wrath being poured out on the unrighteous for a time, their view of God, His love, and His righteous wrath requires that the punishment of hell not go beyond what they deem right or necessary.

It is at this point that we must remind ourselves that we do not have the authority to redefine God's love or to pit it against His other attributes, as though they were not harmonious. Nor do we have the right to redefine the duration of hell if it does not fit our opinions. As we have seen in previous chapters, God is love. All of His actions (wrath included) define love and how true love acts. Furthermore, He is righteous and good in all of His actions, including in the eternal duration of divine punishment of the wicked in hell. Since God, as the only being who possesses all of the knowledge needed to make a fair and right judgment, has revealed in Scripture that the unrighteous 'will pay the penalty of eternal destruction' (2 Thess. 2:9) in their 'eternal

10   Ibid., 165.
11   Ibid., 166.

torment' (Matt. 25:46) for their sins against Him, then that is the right allotment of punishment they will endure. This punishment will be right, just, fair, and in accordance to God's nature (as I have attempted to show in previous chapters), including His love. If we redefine God's love based on our own view of love and what such love does and does not do, we redefine God over and against how He has revealed Himself. Therefore, we should be cautious before attacking God, His love, or the eternality of hell, since we tend to lack the divine perspective needed in this important topic.

THE JUSTICE OBJECTION

Some annihilationists maintain that, no matter how wicked someone is in an earthly lifetime, no one *deserves* eternal punishment. In other words, a finite number of sins against God should not mandate an infinite punishment. They claim that the punishment is too much for the crime committed and that eternal punishment would not be true justice. Rather, they would see eternal punishment as divine cruelty and injustice carried out by the very One who is supposed to dispense true justice. Thus some annihilationists see hell's eternality as an endless 'torture chamber' rather than as justice. Since this goes against their understanding of God's character, they reject eternal punishment. We will answer this objection in three ways. First, we will uphold the Bible's declaration of hell as eternal as we admit that our finite and fallen perspectives hinder us in understanding justice truly. Second, we will think through how a fallen nature acts against God throughout the duration of eternity. Third, we will examine justice from the perspective of Christ's victory over His enemies.

First, let us think about justice from our own finite and fallen perspectives. We are finite creatures and therefore limited in understanding, knowledge, and time. Our fallen sense of justice is in line with the definition of justice that best fits the culture of our own day. In other words, we can view justice only from a small slice of life that is relegated to our own awareness. Since our sense of justice does not line up universally with other cultures throughout history, we should be cautious in proclaiming that we are the sole possessors of what is true and sensible justice. The writings of other cultures in other times certainly disagree with current American or global justice. The same will most likely hold true for many other modern cultures and their definitions of justice. Therefore, we would be wise to refrain from stating what God should and should not do in the future as He dispenses justice in hell. Furthermore, attempts to force God into our current and fluctuating sense of justice are shortsighted. He alone has one standard that never changes due to times or seasons. Politics or political theory will never alter His sense of justice. He will always have one standard of justice, and He will never violate that standard.

We must also admit that we are sinful. Our thoughts and opinions on most matters tend to change because our own hearts can be hardened and contrary to God and His ways. We are selfish creatures who put ourselves and our needs before God. We view God's actions in heaven and hell based on what we want Him to do rather than on what He should do based on His own holy nature. When we admit our own sinful tendencies, we should also admit that we possess neither the aptitude nor the perspective to say what true justice is. Our fallen definitions of justice will always be just that—fallen and shortsighted.

Since we lack the ability to know the true depth of sin, we should be cautious in using hyperbolic phrases to describe what seems to be excessive punishment in hell. What is the right amount of punishment for those who sin against an infinitely holy and righteous God? Since all created things lack the essential divine qualities (and perspective) to make this determination rightly, we cannot on our own know for certain what is true justice for a lifetime of sins against God. What we can agree with is the fact that God is righteous and just. He will never commit a sin in His own being or actions. If He were to carry out an unjust punishment, it would violate His nature. It is this knowledge that allows us the ability to know that no unjust punishment will ever transpire in hell. When He created hell, He did so with a purpose of carrying out universal justice against the unrighteous. Even in the eternal duration of hell, God will never be excessive.

Second, let us consider the justice of eternal punishment in light of our natures. The Bible says that we all possess fallen, sinful natures. In other words, by nature we are all 'dead in trespasses and sins' (Eph. 2:1) and are 'by nature children of wrath' (v. 3). This means that unless God changes our natures, we will always sin against Him by breaking His holy laws. For such sin, He will always respond in wrath. The Bible also says that the only way anyone can leave this fallen nature is by God's regenerating us (or making us born again). It is only in this new regenerated nature that we have the ability not to sin against God. Furthermore, the Bible says that when those who are born again are raised in their resurrected bodies in the final judgment, they are 'glorified'. To be glorified means that one's nature, body, and soul are all fully glorified and incapable of sinning against God. This is why those who are granted heaven will be in heaven for eternity. All of heaven's citizens are sealed in their glorified natures and will not (nor cannot) ever sin against God. All of their thoughts and actions will be in right accordance with God and His laws.

This same line of logic now applies to the wicked in hell. The wicked will also receive resurrected bodies at the final judgment. However, they will not be glorified in their natures but rather will remain forever in their fallen natures that can only sin against God for eternity. Thus, in all of their thoughts and actions in hell, they will always and forever sin against Him in the hardness of their hearts. They will never repent nor have the desire to do so. They will be forever 'dead in trespasses and sins' against God. Since this is the case, then the wicked will not merely be paying for a finite number of sins committed during life but will also be punished for their continual sins against God into eternity. They will forever gnash their teeth against God and His holiness because they will be forever dead in their fallen sinful natures. There will never be a moment in eternity in which they will obey, or even desire to obey, God. Thus they will forever and constantly sin against Him. Seen from this perspective, it is sensible that God's punishment for eternal sin would in fact be eternal punishment.

Third, let us look at the justice of God's eternal punishment in light of the complete victory of Jesus Christ. The book of Hebrews describes Jesus as the special Son of God who is the eternal King who loves righteousness (Heb. 1:8-9), the Creator of the world who laid the foundation of the earth and the heavens, the One who receives service and worship from the angels (1:6), the eternal God who outlasts the original heavens and earth (1:11), the One who ends this age and inaugurates the age to come (1:12), and the

One who will have His enemies under His feet (1:13; 2:8; 10:13).

When it comes to *when* the Son will have all of His enemies under His feet, we look at Hebrews 1:13 and 2:8. In 1:13 we read: 'Sit at My right hand, until I make Your enemies a footstool for Your feet.' The New Testament teaches that the moment Jesus ascended to heaven, He was at the Father's right hand. The Bible also teaches that Jesus will remain with His Father until His Second Coming, or return. Then He will execute the final judgment, in which all people will be judged according to their relationship to Him. Those with faith in Christ will be granted eternal life in heaven and will receive God's eternal covenant blessings. Those without faith in Christ will receive eternal death and punishment in hell.

As we have also seen in chapters 3–4 of this book, Jesus is not only present in hell but is also carrying out God's wrath against His enemies. This imagery of Christ's punishing His enemies is of His final victory over them. Put another way, as Christ carries out the wrath of God against His enemies, it can also be said that His enemies are under His feet in subjection to Him (Heb. 2:8) as a footstool (1:13; 10:13). In this current age, we do not see this final and ultimate subjection to Jesus of His enemies, because Hebrews 2:8 indicates that this subjection will be in the future: 'You have put all things in subjection under His feet. For in subjecting all things to him, He left nothing that is not subject to Him. But now we do not yet see all things subjected to Him.' When will we see this final and ultimate subjection of Christ's enemies? It seems that the Bible states that final judgment and eternal punishment in hell will be this ultimate subjection, as Christ's enemies will be punished forever for their constant and continual sin against God.

As we have already seen, hell is not a place that ceases to be once God brings about the new heavens and the new earth. Rather, Revelation 21:1-9 shows that hell, as a lake of fire, is part of that new creation and will continue to exist throughout eternity. The lake of fire is where God will punish each of those whose 'name was not found written in the book of life' (Rev. 20:15), those who are 'unbelieving and abominable and murderers and immoral persons and sorcerers and idolaters and all liars' (21:8), along with the Devil, the beast, the false prophet 'day and night forever and ever' (20:10). It is assumed that the 'smoke of their torment' (14:11) that goes up forever and ever will be seen from the high mountaintop that will be the New Jerusalem (21:10), where those whose names are written in the Lamb's book of life will spend eternity (21:27). If this is true, then the saints of God will be able to praise God for His marvelous and gracious works in the New Jerusalem and at the same time witness the rising smoke of the torment of those in the lake of fire. In this way, we will see the eternal subjection of Christ's enemies underneath His feet.

These enemies will remain Christ's enemies for eternity as they are forever in their fallen natures. In other words, there will not be a time when their selfishness or idolatry will cease. They will continue on as God's enemies and thus will continually break God's laws in their fallen natures.[12] The fact that they remain enemies of God for eternity means that they have not and will not stop sinning against God. Thus we might deduce that even as they are being punished for eternity, these enemies of Christ will still love themselves more than God and will rail against Him as they 'gnash their teeth' against God in anger. Therefore, we assume that their punishment will continue for eternity in hell because their sin will continue throughout eternity in hell.

THE LANGUAGE OBJECTION

Some annihilationists look at some of the specific language the Bible uses to describe hell in order to buttress their position. The main words that annihilationists tend to focus on in order to create an alternative to eternal punishment are 'destroy', 'death', and 'eternal'. For the purpose of this

---

12   Carson, 'On Banishing the Lake of Fire', 533.

book, we will make only a limited study of the word group that includes 'to destroy', 'to lose', and 'to perish'.[13]

DESTRUCTION/KILL/PERISH

The annihilationist camp is right to show that God's punishment in hell is total destruction. We have already made this claim and defined what these words mean throughout the New Testament in chapters 3–4. However, annihilationists claim that the word group of 'destroy', 'perish', 'lose', and 'kill' can mean that whatever is destroyed in hell is destroyed to the point of non-existence. In other words, annihilationists maintain that this word group equates to 'destroyed so that the object no longer exists.' In this assumption they have made an error that oversteps the contextual meaning of these words.

In the Gospels, 'to destroy' or 'destruction' comes from these Greek words and their derivatives: *apollumi, aphanizō, kataluō, diaphtherō, luō, olethreuō, portheō,* and *kathaireō*. In order to make a clear case that none of these words requires annihilation in the Bible, we will work through a few of

---

13 As well as Carson ('On Banishing the Lake of Fire', 515-35), the
    following have already covered word groups such as fire, eternal,
    death: Christopher W. Morgan and Robert A. Peterson (eds), *Hell
    Under Fire*, (Grand Rapids, MI: Zondervan, 2004); Eryl Davies,
    'Hell: More Objections Considered', in Eryl Davies, *An Angry
    God? What the Bible Says About Wrath, Final Judgment, and Hell*
    (Bryntirion, Bridgend: Wales: Evangelical Press of Wales, 1991),
    132-45.

their uses in the Gospels to see what they mean. For sake of space, we will not carry out this exercise for the rest of the New Testament, since the point we are making should become obvious.

DESTROY: TO KILL OR DIE

In this section we will see that the majority of passages containing this word group include the idea of death but in no way require annihilation.[14] In Matthew 2:13 we are told that King Herod is trying to find the child Jesus in order to destroy (*apollumi*) him. In other words, Herod is trying to kill or end the life of the child Jesus. Let us imagine for a moment that Herod was successful in carrying out this destruction. While the child might be dead, the body would still exist for a time even as decomposition transpired. Furthermore, the soul would still be in existence. I make this point in order to show that the Bible does not demand that 'destroy' requires annihilation to the point of non-existence. This same idea is found in Matthew 8:25 (see also Mark 4:38; Luke 8:24); 12:14 (see also Mark 11:18; Luke 19:27); 22:7; 26:52; and Luke 17:26-27.

In Luke 4:33-34 a demon-possessed man confronts Jesus, and the demon says, 'Let us alone! What business do we

---

14 For a fuller response to the language objection see Moo's exegetical and language arguments against annihilationism in Douglas J. Moo, 'Paul on Hell', in Morgan and Peterson (eds), *Hell Under Fire*, 92-109.

have with each other, Jesus of Nazareth? Have You come to destroy [*apollumi*] us? I know who You are—the Holy One of God!' It seems as though the demon understands that Jesus is the One who will carry out the demon's destruction in hell. But this destruction is not annihilation. We know this to be the case as we read this passage in light of others. In Matthew 8:29 two demons cry out, 'What business do we have with each other, Son of God? Have You come to torment us before the time?' In Mark 5:7 the demon-possessed man cries, 'What business do we have with each other, Jesus, Son of the Most High God? I implore You by God, do not torment me!' The demons seem to understand that there will be a time in which Jesus will carry out their torment and destruction. The two ideas must be seen together as the unending divine punishment that all demons will receive in hell. In other words, the demons are destroyed by being continually punished in hell by the Son of God in the second death, just as the book of Revelation describes: 'The smoke of their torment goes up forever and ever; they have no rest day and night, those who worship the beast and his image, and whoever receives the mark of his name' (Rev. 14:11).[15] The demons do not have any sort of annihilation in view.

---

15 Robert W. Yarbrough, 'Jesus on Hell', in Morgan and Peterson (eds), *Hell Under Fire*, 81.

Perhaps Matthew 10:28 is the strongest case for annihilationism—if this passage were the only one in the Bible to speak about the duration of hell. It reads: 'Do not fear those who kill the body but are unable to kill the soul; rather fear Him who is able to destroy [*apollumi*] both the soul and body in hell.' In context, Jesus is encouraging His disciples to preach the gospel without fear of persecution or suffering even to the point of death. They will face pain and suffering as they preach the gospel. But the fear of pain and suffering should not keep them from their duties. After all, death in the Christian context is not the final chapter, since one continues to live in soul at the moment of death and in body and soul in heaven after the final judgment. Thus Jesus bolsters their confidence by reminding them that God is the One who will punish and destroy the wicked in hell.

If this were the only passage in the entire Bible to speak about hell as the place where God is able to destroy both body and soul, then it might fit with the annihilationist program. However, since we have already established the fact that hell is the place of eternal punishment through various Scriptures, we are not allowed to redefine the duration of hell based on a nuanced reading of one passage. Rather, this passage must fit with the rest of the Bible's clear teaching on hell as eternal punishment. Thus we should understand destruction here to be 'God's punishment of the ungodly with forfeiture of all that is worthwhile in human existence'[16] in hell.

Moreover, we should also note that Jesus is speaking about a total punishment in hell. In hell, one does not suffer merely bodily but rather in totality in body and soul. In other words, there is no portion of the human being that does not suffer eternal punishment in hell. Understood in this manner, the passage places teeth in the warning that Jesus is seeking to give. To claim that evildoers will suffer only for a limited time before being annihilated out of existence seems to be the exact opposite of what Jesus is trying to accomplish in this passage.[17]

LOSE: LOSS OF VALUE

In Matthew 5:29-30 Jesus warns His disciples to avoid sin at all costs:

> If your right eye makes you stumble, tear it out and throw it away from you; for it is better for you to lose [*apollumi*] one of the parts of your body, than for your whole body to be thrown into hell. If your right hand makes you stumble, cut it off and throw it from you; for it is better for you to lose [*apollumi*] one of the parts of your body than for your whole body to go into hell.

---

16 Robert A. Peterson, *Hell on Trial: The Case for Eternal Punishment* (P & R Publishing Co., 1995), 44-5.

17 See Robert W. Yarbrough, 'Jesus on Hell', 80, as he works through this same passage against annihilationist Edward Fudge.

With this descriptive language Jesus is creating a contrast of pain and loss. On one hand, there is temporal pain and loss in this life, seen here in the loss of an eye or the amputation of a limb. This pain would be severe, but it has limitations. On the other hand, the pain and loss that will be felt in hell will not have a limit. It will be an unending pain felt in both body and soul (Matt. 10:28) and will be eternal (25:46).

Apollumi can also mean to ruin something totally. In Matthew 9:16-17 (see also Mark 2:22; Luke 5:37) Jesus uses this verb to indicate that a garment and a wineskin can be ruined: 'No one puts a patch of unshrunk cloth on an old garment; for the patch pulls away from the garment, and a worse tear results. Nor do people put new wine into old wineskins; otherwise the wineskins burst, and the wine pours out and the wineskins are ruined [*apollumi*]; but they put new wine into new wineskins, and both are preserved.' If one is not careful, an old garment can be ruined (*apollumi*) without proper repair. The same holds true when new wine bursts and ruins (*apollumi*) an old wineskin. Both items can be described as ruined or destroyed since they are useless for their intended usage. However, as D. A. Carson notes: 'In neither case is cessation of existence in view.'[18]

---

18   D. A. Carson, 'On Banishing the Lake of Fire', 522.

The same idea can be seen in Luke 15:1-32. In this long passage Jesus references a lost (*apollumi*) sheep, a lost (*apollumi*) coin, and a lost (*apollumi*) son. In each case the item is lost (*apollumi*) for a moment. However, each item is still in existence and simply needs to be located. In the case of the lost sheep the shepherd searches the open pasture until he locates what was lost (*apollumi*). In the case of the lost coin (*apollumi*) the woman searches her house until she finds that which was previously lost (*apollumi*). And, in the case of the lost son, when the son returns to his father's house, he was 'lost and has been found' (Luke 15:32). *Apollumi* in these cases cannot be seen as annihilating from existence, since each item is simply lost but later is found.[19]

CONCLUSION ON THE WORD GROUP FOR DESTROY/KILL/ LOST

In all of these uses in the Gospel accounts, there is not a single instance in which these passages require a meaning of annihilation or cessation from existence. Not only do the Gospels not require annihilation as a meaning, but destruction as extinction is a foreign and unwelcome intrusion upon the clear and lucid teaching of the Gospels. Since no apostle would ever contradict his Master, Jesus, we can safely assume that the rest of the New Testament

---

19 Douglas J. Moo, 'Paul on Hell', in Morgan and Peterson (eds), *Hell Under Fire*, 105.

findings from this word group will yield similar results to this brief study. No matter how one feels about the nature of eternal punishment in hell, we cannot reinterpret the Bible to incorporate annihilationism. Thus we cannot accept annihilationism or any of its derivatives.

Will the wicked be destroyed, be killed, and suffer the second death in hell? The answer is an obvious yes. The unrighteous will be eternally destroyed and come to total ruin and loss, as their function in life comes to nothing but divine wrath. Instead of being creatures who rightly serve their Creator in continual worship in heaven, they will have lost their life calling and will suffer eternal wrath while never ceasing to exist in hell.

THE PHILOSOPHICAL OBJECTION

Many annihilationists, specifically from the conditional camp, claim that the human soul is not immortal.[20] Thus they argue that, once the body and soul are destroyed (again, conditionalists assume destruction to the point of annihilation), there is nothing left of the individual to receive God's eternal punishment.

Moreover, annihilationists claim that the only way one could hold to conscious eternal punishment would be if

---

20 Edward William Fudge, 'Souls: Immortal or Otherwise', in Edward William Fudge, *The Fire that Consumes: A Biblical and Historical Study of the Doctrine of Final Punishment*, 3rd edition (Eugene, OR: Wipf & Stock, 2011), 19-32.

the human soul were immortal. They also claim that early Christians borrowed and assumed the immortality of the soul from Plato's philosophy.[21] Therefore, annihilationists state that the body and soul are destroyed to the point of annihilation in hell.

This line of thinking does not quite fit the picture that the Bible portrays for humanity, nor what the historical view of hell teaches.

First, annihilationists are correct to state that the human soul is not essentially immortal. God alone is immortal, and humans are not divine. Thus it is correct to state that we do not possess by nature an immortal soul.

If we do not possess an immortal soul, then how can anyone live forever, either in heaven with eternal life or in hell with eternal death? In order for us to live forever, God must grant us that aspect of eternality. In John 5:21-22 Jesus declares: 'Just as the Father raised the dead and gives them life, even so the Son also gives life to whom He wishes. For not even the Father judges anyone, but He has given all judgment over to the Son.' Here, we must admit that if eternal life is obtained, for either heaven or hell, it must be given to us by God as the One who gives life to those raised from the dead.

---

21   Ibid., 19.

Now the question is, who will God raise from the dead? Will He only raise believers to eternal life? Or will He also raise the wicked to eternality as well? John 5:28-29 says: 'Do not marvel at this; for an hour is coming, in which all who are in the tombs will hear His voice and will come forth; those who did the good deeds to a resurrection of life, those who committed the evil deeds to a resurrection of judgment.' At this point, we must admit that God will call all people everywhere to a general resurrection from the dead so that He can declare and bring final judgment.

For those who are believers in Jesus Christ, it is clear that God grants them immortality and a resurrected body so that they might endure God's unadulterated glory for eternity (2 Tim. 1:10). On this point, the annihilationists agree with the historic view.

But what about those who are sentenced and sent to hell? Does God give them eternality and a resurrected body so that they might endure His punishment for eternity? While there are no scriptural verses that come right out and make this claim, I think we can connect the dots with a clear conscience. We are certain that God will resurrect the wicked for the final judgment (John 5:29). And, as Christopher Morgan notes, God will sustain those in hell for eternity:

It seems clear from Revelation 20:10 as well that Satan, the beast, and the false prophet are punished forever. Do they somehow have an inherent immortality? Of course not.

God will keep them in existence endlessly in order to punish them. Similarly, the wicked will be punished consciously forever in hell, not because they exist as immortal souls but because God will sustain them.[22]

The logic is sound. If there are people in hell (and the Bible is very clear that there will be), and hell is where God punishes His enemies for eternity (which is the clear teaching of the Bible and has been accepted as such since the early Church), then it stands that God will grant those enemies eternality and sustain them during their punishment.

Does the Bible teach Annihilationism?

We should conclude that the Bible does not teach annihilationism in any capacity. The Bible provides several pictures of the nature and duration of hell. It is where the enemies of God will spend eternity in conscious punishment. It will be a place of pain, separation from God's heavenly city, and banishment from the light of His covenant blessings, where the wicked will be eternally destroyed and brought to total ruin by Jesus Christ but will never cease to exist in the second death that lasts forever and ever.

Hebrews 6:2 teaches the importance of eternal judgment: to fight against hell's eternality is to attempt to fight against an elementary truth. In other words, to offer up an explanation,

---

22 Christopher W. Morgan, 'Annihilationism: Will the Unsaved Be Punished Forever?' in Morgan and Peterson (eds), *Hell Under Fire*, 205.

or prospect, that hell is temporary in any fashion is to work against one of Christianity's foundational truths. Scripture is offering a proper warning at this point: 'Do not mess this teaching up', or else we will distort various truths and end up with something that does not resemble biblical truth.

7

Is Hell Emptied?

If we are not careful to maintain a right focus on the nature and character of God as the starting point of theological questions, we can easily slip into error in several areas. In fact, if we approach a theological issue from anything other than a balanced and biblical view of God, we face the high likelihood of making a mistake.

If we approach the subject of sin from the standpoint of culture and humanity, we will not understand sin rightly. Sin must be seen in light of the One whom sin offends. Sin must be defined in light of God. Sin's punishment must be defined in that same light.

The same holds true for the wider discussion on hell. If we do not maintain a careful balance concerning *all* of God's attributes at the same time, we run the risk of understanding hell in a manner contrary to how it is described in the Bible.

For some people (such as Friedrich Schleiermacher), God's love is the primary and main attribute that defines Him and drives His actions. In this understanding, God's love seems to override His other attributes, such as holiness or justice, to the extent that God saves all people everywhere without exception, either immediately or ultimately. According to this type of universalism, hell will be emptied, and all people will eventually end up in heaven.

Furthermore, any discussion on hell must look at the whole picture the Bible gives to us instead of focusing primarily on any one image. If we focus too much on the total and complete victory of Christ over His enemies but fail to see that Jesus Himself clearly states that there are people in hell (and will be for eternity), we have misunderstood what this vast and complete victory entails. While for some this might be more pleasant to think about than the reality the Bible paints, we must return to the complete and holistic portrait drawn from the totality of the Bible. The Bible teaches that there are people in hell, and will be for eternity.

In this chapter, we will briefly examine the false hope of universalism.

WHAT IS UNIVERSALISM?

Universalism maintains that God will ultimately save all people from all time periods without exception. God's universal salvation of all people will be so successful that heaven will be filled with every human being who has ever lived. At the same time, it also means that hell will be completely empty in the end.

According to this view, no matter what people do in this life, no matter how they live, God's love will ultimately drive all people to Himself, and all people will be saved. This means that the kind (or unkind, for that matter) atheist down the street will be in heaven. This means that the Pol Pots, Joseph Stalins, and Adolf Hitlers of the world will be in heaven. It also means that every terrorist, suicide bomber, rapist, and child molester will be admitted to God's heaven. In other words, one's actions in this life, no matter how wicked, do not matter, since all people everywhere will reap the reward of heaven.

While the main tenet of universal salvation is granted in all forms and branches of universalism, there are varying degrees of thought within this wide-ranging camp. For our purposes, we cannot work through every distinct movement but will restrict ourselves to those who have held to universalism on biblical or theological grounds.[1]

Within the various camps of universalism, there are some groups who think that hell is merely a hypothetical warning

---

1   Or what Hart calls 'Christian Universalism'; see Trevor Hart, 'Universalism: Two Distinct Types', in Nigel M. de S. Cameron *Universalism and the Doctrine of Hell: Papers Presented at the Fourth Edinburgh Conference in Christian Dogmatics 1991*, (Carlisle, UK: Paternoster, 1992), 15.

that does not actually exist. Others see hell as a purgatorial place where God applies corrective discipline until the sinner is ready for heaven. In other words, God's wrath is neither punitive nor eternal in these versions of universalism.

HOW DO UNIVERSALISTS ARRIVE AT THEIR POSITION?

A BRIEF HISTORY OF UNIVERSALISM[2]

Some historians assert that Clement of Alexandria (A.D. 150–220) was the first early church thinker to teach a form of universalism.[3] This is debatable.

However, Clement's student Origen of Alexandria (A.D. 185–254) is the first early Church father to create an unmistakable theory of Christian universalism. His theory is called *apokatastasis*, or the 'restoration' of all things. In Origen's view, Acts 3:19-21 teaches that all things will be restored to an Eden-like state in which all creation has repented (Satan, demons, and humans alike) and therefore resides with God in perfect fellowship for eternity:

> Therefore repent and turn, so that your sins may be wiped away, in order that times of refreshing may come from the presence of the Lord; and that He may send Jesus, the Christ appointed for you, whom heaven must receive until the period of restoration

---

2   For a more thorough history see Richard Bauckham, 'Universalism: A Historical Survey', *Themelios* 4/2 (September 1978): 47-54.

3   Robert A. Morey, *Death and the Afterlife* (Minneapolis: Bethany, 1984), 223.

[*apokatastasis*] of all things about which God spoke by
the mouth of His holy prophets from ancient time.

This perspective contains a serious problem, as the Bible clearly teaches that Satan, his demons, and all people without faith in Christ are cast into the lake of fire (hell) for eternity (Rev. 20:10–21:8). Thus the fact that the Bible teaches that there will be people in hell for eternity seems to disprove this vein of universalism (more on that later in this chapter). Moreover, Acts 3 goes on to state: 'And it will be that every soul that does not heed that prophet [Jesus Christ] shall be utterly destroyed from among the people' (Acts 3:23). This well-known passage clearly teaches that all people who are not found to be righteous through the Son, Jesus Christ, will be punished in hell. It does not say that those in hell will be cleansed or purified and then allowed into heaven. Origen's particular brand of universalism runs contrary to the Bible and has been denounced as heresy throughout church history.

Other than in a few isolated cases, universalism did not make much of a sound until after the Reformation. Even though church confessions have continued to denounce the teaching as contrary to the clear teaching of the Bible, universalism has gained more and more acceptance in recent centuries. In the nineteenth century, Friedrich Schleiermacher taught that the entire human race was elected into the saving work of Christ and would therefore be saved. Twentieth-century theologians Karl Barth and Emil Brunner have been labeled as universalists but probably do not deserve this badge, as they both taught what J. I. Packer calls the 'pious hope' of universal salvation.[4] In other words, while they created a theological picture of universalism, they did not commit to the movement in its entirety.

Modern universalists include Nels Ferré of Sweden and John A. T. Robinson of England. Ferré became a universalist through a reshaping of the doctrine of God (see below) and stated that heaven and hell could not exist together since they are opposed to one another: 'If eternal hell is real, love is eternally frustrated and heaven is a place of mourning and concern for the lost. Such joy and grief cannot go together. There can be no psychiatric split personality for the real lovers of God and surely not for God himself.'[5]

Robinson picks up where Origen left off in a desire for full restoration of all people: 'Christ, in Origen's old words, remains on the cross so long as one sinner remains in hell. That is not speculation: it is a statement grounded in the very necessity of God's nature. In a universe of love there

---

4   J. I. Packer, 'Universalism: Will Everyone Ultimately Be Saved?' in Morgan and Peterson (eds), *Hell Under Fire*, 172-3.

5   Nels Ferré, *The Christian Understanding of God* (New York: Harper & Brothers, 1951), 237.

can be no heaven which tolerates a chamber of horrors.'[6] This brand of universalism seems to stem from a singular focus on the love of God rather than a holistic view of God. It maintains that unless there is a noble conclusion for all people, God has failed by allowing evil to triumph.[7]

UNIVERSALISM AND THE DOCTRINE OF GOD

Many universalists tend to start with a particular approach to God's love. While universalists certainly affirm the holiness and righteousness of God, they suggest that the love of God is the overarching and dominating attribute that shapes and determines the outcome of all the others. Thus, the love of God dictates how and when God can show His righteousness and justice. In this line of thinking, universalists might turn to 1 John 4:8, 16 to state that 'God is love'. Instead of allowing God's love to be defined by God's actions, however, they redefine God's love for Him from their own perspectives. They tend to create a picture of love that God must uphold and live up to or else be labeled as 'unloving'. In the case of universalism, they demand that true divine love must ensure that all people everywhere ultimately end up in heaven. Furthermore, they might move from the love of God to His loving desire to save all people: 'God …

6   J. A. T. Robinson, *In the End, God: A Study of the Christian Doctrine of Last Things* (Eugene, OR: Cascade, 2011), 116.

7   John Hick, *Death and Eternal Life* (London: Collins, 1976), 258-9. Hick eventually added pluralism to his universalism.

desires all men to be saved and to come to the knowledge of the truth' (1 Tim. 2:4). Finally, some universalists have turned to 2 Peter 3:9 to show how the loving God displays patience so that all people might be saved: 'The Lord is not slow about His promise, as some count slowness, but is patient toward you, not wishing for any to perish but for all to come to repentance.'

Before we turn to each of these passages to interpret what they mean in context, we must first remind ourselves of how we are to view God through His attributes. Just as we saw in chapter 2, God most certainly is love. He is the very definition of love. When we look at God, we must see His actions—past, present, and future—as the very definition of *authentic* love. There is nothing in God or His divine plans that cannot be defined as real love. But He does not work merely in love to the exclusion of His other attributes. He does not 'turn off' His holiness so that He can be loving. He cannot shed Himself of His righteousness in order to love more people. Therefore, we must remember that there is no single attribute that drives the rest of God's attributes. He is all of His divine attributes at the same time. God is love. God is holy. God is righteous. God is just. God is all of these things equally and at the same time for every moment throughout eternity.

Furthermore, we must take extreme caution in forcing our view of love on God. When we make statements like,

'If the cries of hell exist while there is praise in heaven, then God has failed and heaven is not truly heaven', we are making the mistake of forcing our views of God and His love onto Him. Again, we have to remember that we are fallen and sinful. Thus our thoughts and opinions on love vacillate and differ depending on circumstances or context. As such, our fallen views of love cannot determine God's love. Rather, God's actions must determine how we should see love. Since the Bible shows that this loving God has placed heaven and hell alongside one another in the new creation, we should understand that we cannot rewrite the script in order to create a future we prefer. In other words, the perfect Creator gets to define love for the creation, rather than the other way around.

God alone is right, holy, and just at all times and in all ways. He is also love. If God, in His love and holiness, demands eternal punishment in hell for sins committed against Him, perhaps we should seek His established means of escape through Jesus Christ rather than painting a new picture on a new canvas. The fact that Revelation 21:1-8 shows people in both heaven and hell in God's new creation for eternity demonstrates the truth of the matter. Hell exists for eternity, and the people in hell will pay for their sins for eternity. This truth should prove to us that universalism cannot be accurate. Furthermore, we must come to understand that the existence of hell does not mean that God is anything less than flawless love. God is love, and He has created a place where He will carry out justice for eternity. Both of these facts are true at the same time.

1 JOHN 4:8, 16 AND GOD'S LOVE

First John 4:8, 16 do indeed say that 'God is love'. But do these verses intend to create a doctrine of universal salvation *because* God is love? Are universalists right to start here in 1 John 4 as the foundation of universalism? In order to answer that question, let us take a closer look at what John says.

These verses must be seen in their proper context. John is writing to believers to warn them against false teaching. He says: 'Beloved [a term for those who already have faith in Jesus Christ], do not believe every spirit, but test the spirits to see whether they are from God, because many false prophets have gone out into the world' (1 John 4:1). John goes on to state that those teachers who lift up the truth of Jesus Christ and a love for one another are speaking truth. These prophets are speaking rightly. Those who, on the other hand, do not advise believers to love God and one another are not from God. This is because 'the one who does not love does not know God, for God is love' (v. 8). Again, John says:

> We have come to know and have believed the love which God has for us. God is love and the one who abides in love abides in God, and God abides in him. By this, love is perfected with us, so that we may have confidence in the day of judgment; because as He is,

> so also are we in this world… If someone says, 'I love God' and hates his brother, he is a liar, for the one who does not love his brother whom he has seen, cannot love God whom he has not seen (1 John 4:16-20).

This passage cannot teach universalism, as its aim is to teach the opposite. This passage is a warning to those who do not love God and neighbor. John is saying, quite clearly, that if one does not love God in Christ rightly and does not love one's neighbor through Christ, then that person is not in Christ or in God. If someone is not in Christ, he *should* fear God on the day of judgment, knowing that he will face divine wrath for law-breaking. Moreover, those who teach something other than the need to love God and neighbor rightly are false teachers. As false teachers, they should not only expect wrath on the day of judgment; they should also fear God in anticipation of that day.

Only those who are united to Christ in faith and live out their commitment to Him through love can be assured that they are safe from falling into divine wrath in hell.

Most important is what John writes between these verses. While universalists seek to maintain that God's love will not end in wrath, this very passage defines God's love through the wrath that He has poured out on God the Son, Jesus Christ. First John 4:10 declares: 'In this is love, not that we loved God, but that He loved us and sent His Son to be the propitiation for our sins.' God's love *cannot* be discussed rightly outside of His dealings with sin. Since God is just, holy, and righteous, His amazing love was displayed when His Son, Jesus Christ, became the sin substituted and paid the just penalty of God's wrath for all who believe in Jesus. But this loving act of propitiation is not applied to those who are not united to Jesus by faith. Thus there remains an eternal divine wrath that will be applied to all who are not found united by faith to Christ.

While these verses do say that 'God is love', we are not allowed to take these words and create our own meaning behind them. The context and flow of the passage will always define such words for us. Moreover, once the right meaning is established, we do not have the authority to change it in any way. Thus, while we can certainly agree with universalists that God is love, we should take great caution before using these verses as a means to teach that God saves all people everywhere.

2 Peter 3:9 and God's desire and patience

Does 2 Peter 3:9 truly teach or imply that God will save all people everywhere? When we look at this verse in context, we must note several features. First, this letter is written to 'those who have received a faith of the same kind as ours, by the righteousness of our God and Savior, Jesus Christ' (2 Pet. 1:1) for the purpose of 'seeing that His divine power has granted to us everything pertaining to life and godliness, through the true knowledge of Him who called us by His own glory and excellence' (v. 3). In other words, this letter is written to those who are already believers in Jesus Christ but need to be encouraged in their faith in the midst of false teaching.

Second, Peter assures these Christians that those who are teaching falsely will face 'swift destruction' and condemnation from God on the day of final judgment (2 Pet. 2:1-9). In 2 Peter 3:7 Peter recounts that God has kept the heavens and the earth ready 'for the day of judgment and destruction of ungodly men'. Moreover, God has promised that all false teachers will be judged 'to their own destruction' (3:16). Peter is clear that hell will be filled with those who are false teachers and try to derail Christians in their pursuit of Christ (see chapter 4 of this book).

It is in this light that Peter says to those who are struggling to shrug off false teaching that God desires that they (specifically those who already believe in Jesus Christ but are struggling to hold to true teaching) not give in to false teaching and perish but instead come to repentance (2 Pet. 3:9). Far from teaching universal salvation to all humanity, this passage in context teaches that God desires that His people keep the faith, knowing that all false teachers and ungodly men will be judged and punished in hell.

Philippians 2:9-11 and Christ's victory over His enemies

Some universalists argue that Christ's victory on the cross in Philippians 2:9-11 demonstrates that all people will ultimately come to saving faith in Him. Some universalists maintain that Christ's saving work on the cross atones for all of the sins of all people in the world and displays His ultimate victory over His enemies to the point that they all come to Him in faith. In speaking of Christ's conquest this passage states: 'For this reason also, God highly exalted him, and bestowed on Him the name which is above every name, so that at the name of Jesus every knee will bow, of those who are in heaven and on earth and under the earth, and that every tongue confess that Jesus Christ is Lord, to the glory of God the Father.'

At first glance, this passage does perhaps seem to represent a universal salvation. After all, those in heaven and on the earth will bow the knee to Jesus and confess that He is Lord. But the text also says that those 'under the earth' will do the same. Does this language imply that those who are being punished right now 'under the earth' will ultimately come to a saving confession in Jesus Christ? Will they come to Jesus and bow their knees in worship of the Son of God as proof of their newfound faith?

First, we ought to notice that Paul is quoting an Old Testament passage in Philippians 2:10. Thus we must consider the original passage, discover its meaning, and note how its context relates to Philippians 2.

This quotation is from Isaiah 45:22-25, which carries the meaning needed to understand Philippians 2:9-11 rightly. It reads:

> Turn to Me and be saved, all the ends of the earth; for I am God, and there is no other. I have sworn by Myself, the word has gone forth from My mouth in righteousness and will not turn back, that to Me every knee will bow, every tongue will swear. They will say of Me, 'Only in the Lord are righteousness and strength.' Men will come to Him, and all who were angry at Him will be put to shame. In the Lord all of the offspring of Israel will be justified and will glory.

In Isaiah 44–45 God speaks of how He will bring about a universal conquest so that the entire world will know that He alone is God and alone is sovereign over all peoples and nations. He will lead His messenger to an amazing conquest that cannot be questioned. When that conquest is completed, there will be a call to His enemies, offering them a chance to be saved: 'Turn to Me and be saved, all the ends of the earth; for I am God and there is no other' (Isa. 45:22). Next God makes a promise in pure righteousness and swears by it by His most holy name: 'To Me every knee will bow, every tongue will swear' that the Lord alone is righteous and in Him alone is pure strength (vv. 23-24). The next line shows that some will take God up on His offer of salvation: 'Men will come to Him.' In other words, some will come to their conquering God and bow the knee in adoration and worship and swear that He is righteous and strong. In this verse, we do in fact see that God allows His previous enemies to come to Him for salvation.

However, it is the next verse that shows that some will not take Him up on His offer of salvation: 'And all who were angry at Him will be put to shame' (Isa. 45:24b). This group will most certainly still bow the knee, but this will be an act not of worship but of humiliation. They are forced to bow, having been conquered and subdued by God, their opponent. Their tongues will still confess that God is righteous and strong, but it will be a forced confession of a defeated foe, not the glad adoration of a worshiper. This second group is not a picture of those saved and praising God for His work. Rather, it is a picture of hardhearted, bitter, and conquered warriors who have been captured in battle and are being forced to march with shackles and chains (v. 14). These defeated enemies will be 'put to shame and even humiliated, all of them' (v. 16), as they are forced to bow low in humiliation and subjection: '[They] will bow down to you, they will make supplication to you; "Surely God is with you, and there is none else, no other God" (v. 14).

It is this entire meaning that we bring with us to Philippians 2:9-11. Yes, Jesus Christ is the conquering Lord who defeats all His enemies. Yes, some former enemies of Christ will believe in Him and trust Him as their Lord and Savior in this life. When they call upon Him in saving faith, He will be faithful to save them, because He is righteous and has sworn by His own holy Name. Thus, on the day of final judgment, this group will gladly come forward in utter adoration and bow before Him in worship and confess with their tongues that He is Lord.

But the second group will harden their hearts, refuse Him, and reject His gracious offer of salvation in this life. This group will still bow the knee to Jesus Christ on the day of judgment, but it will not be out of salvation or worship. It will be in humiliation and subjection to Him. In other words, some will still despise Jesus even as they bow their knees in forced subjection. Some will still have murderous thoughts about their Conqueror even as their tongues confess that He has defeated them. These will not be saved but rather will face the terrible but righteous wrath of the Lamb 'when the Lord Jesus will be revealed from heaven with His mighty angels in flaming fire, dealing out retribution to those who do not know God and to those who do not obey the gospel of our Lord Jesus. These will pay the penalty of eternal destruction by the presence of the Lord and from the glory of His power' (2 Thess. 1:7-9).

Therefore, upon closer inspection, this passage cannot speak of universal salvation, no matter how badly we might desire all people to be saved. There will be a group of people who hear the message of salvation but refuse to accept God's gracious offer. Thus, for those who are 'under the earth', while they will bow the knee and confess God's righteousness and strength, they will do so as they endure God's just punishment in hell. The Bible speaks of that punishment, as this group is cast into the lake of fire for eternity (Revelation 20–21), not merely as a hypothetical reality or as a corrective action but as eternal punishment for sins committed against God.

However, this passage does point out God's gracious love, as He has made salvation possible for His enemies. This is the heart of the gospel: those who are enemies of God and guilty of breaking His righteous laws can, at the hearing of the good news of Jesus Christ, surrender themselves to Him and His Lordship and cry out to Jesus in saving faith. The Bible promises salvation to everyone who, in this life, repents of his or her sins and turns to Jesus. In this way, many (not all) former enemies of God can and will be saved through the victorious work of Jesus Christ.

It is this very picture that shows us what God's new heavens and new earth will look like. In God's perfect new created order, there is clearly a place where His people will worship Him for eternity. This is the place called heaven. At the same time, the Bible clearly depicts (Revelation 21) a place where God will punish His enemies who remain steadfast and resolute in their sins against Him for eternity. This is the place called hell. We must keep ourselves from revising the Bible's understanding of God's new heavens and new earth for any reason.

WHAT ABOUT THE 'ALL' PASSAGES?

The Bible does include a number of passages that use the word 'all' in reference to the work of Christ. The question we must ask and answer is: do the 'all' passages teach universal salvation? If they do, then there is no question that all Bible-believing people should embrace that view. If they do not, however, and the 'all' passages have a different meaning in view and work in concert with the larger storyline of the Bible, then we should jettison universalism and embrace the text's intended meaning. While we do not have the space to examine each of those passages, we will look at Romans 5 shortly.

Before we do so, we must remember a crucial point of clear Bible teaching. The Bible shows us over and over again that there will be people in hell for eternity. Whether we like it or not, this is and must be an accepted fact as seen from the Bible. Jesus says that there are and will be people in hell for eternity. The apostles all taught that there will be people in hell for eternity. Either universalists are wrong or the Bible is wrong .

Furthermore, as we saw in chapter 3, Jesus is the divine Son of God. In His divinity, He is omniscient and therefore knows all things. He speaks from His divine knowledge of fact. Not only does the Son of God know that there will be people in hell, but He also knows who will be in heaven. Thus, before we venture into the 'all' passages, we must recognize that none of them can have a universal salvation meaning since Scripture shows people in hell. No matter what they *seem* to say at first glance, they will not have, nor can they have, universal salvation as their target, for this would contradict other clear Scriptures. In order to understand what each passage means by 'all', we must define what is meant by 'all'.

'ALL' PASSAGES: ROMANS 5:18

Romans 5:18 states: 'As through one transgression of the one there resulted condemnation to all men, even so through one act of righteousness there resulted justification of life to all men.' In this passage, Paul is explaining how Adam is humanity's federal head. In federalism, the person at the top represents all of the people beneath him or her. An example of federal headship might be seen in a feudal illustration. If a king declares war on another king, then the declaring king's entire nation is at war with the other nation. Every individual who is represented by that king will find himself at war because his federal representative has declared war.

In this case, Adam was the federal head of the entire human race. He was our representative in the garden of Eden. In the garden, God entered into a covenant with Adam (and, through Adam, with all of humanity). He gave Adam a clear law that Adam could not violate. If Adam, who at that moment did not have a fallen nature, obeyed that law, then he, and all people he represented, would have been allowed to live in Eden with God in perfect fellowship (Gen. 2). If, however, Adam violated that clear divine law, then he, and the entire human race Adam represented, would bear the punishment for that law-breaking.

Genesis 3 shows how Adam violated God's covenant law. It also shows how God, out of His righteous nature, dispensed justice. In this just punishment, the entire human race is cursed by God as a law-breaking race. One of the covenant curses that fell on humanity was a fallen nature. At that moment, every single human being who would ever be conceived bears a fallen nature. This fallen nature is antagonistic against God and cannot in any capacity please Him or act in a manner of upholding His laws (Rom. 8:1-11). Therefore, every fallen human being is by nature the enemy of God and will be judged as such. Since humanity has a fallen nature and cannot uphold God's laws, there is no hope of salvation for anyone. From humanity's perspective, salvation is impossible. It is in this way that Paul says: 'So then as through one transgression there resulted condemnation to all men ...' He is reminding his readers that it is through Adam's sin that the entire human race is fallen and cannot save itself. Since we are hopelessly dead in sin and trespasses, the only thing awaiting us is death and divine judgment.

But the Bible also says that, since salvation is impossible for the fallen human race, God would accomplish it for us. He sent God the Son, the second person of the Trinity, to add a human nature to His divine nature as the second Adam. As the second Adam, He must be like the first. This means that He was not born or conceived with a fallen sin nature so He could obey God. Jesus also became the second federal head for humanity. In other words, He represented a group of people in all that He accomplished.

Throughout His earthly life, Jesus upheld the laws of God perfectly. In His obedience, He earned righteousness and life as a man. In the divine plan of God, when Jesus went to the cross He did so as the only means by which God can save sinners in a just manner. He accomplished what is known as the 'great exchange'. On the cross, Jesus took all the sins of all the people He represented—past, present, and future—upon Himself and bore the wrath and consequence of their law-breaking. God poured out His wrath upon the sinless Christ, who became accursed by God for those He represented as federal head. In this way, God was and is able to forgive the sins of all the people Jesus represented as federal head.

Moreover, since Jesus was perfectly obedient to God's laws, both actively and passively, He took His earned righteousness and gave it to all of the people He represented as federal head. In other words, Jesus gave His obedience to all of the people He represented so that, on the day of judgment, those who are represented by Him will be seen as both sinless (having their sins forgiven through the sacrifice of Jesus Christ) and righteous (through the obedience of Jesus given to His people). In this way, Jesus earned eternal life for His people, since they are now seen by God as righteous as well as forgiven. All of these benefits are given as a free gift to all whom Christ represents as federal head. It is applied to them at the very moment they come to Jesus Christ in saving faith. Since all of the people Jesus represents have forgiveness of sins and righteousness according to God's law, they cannot be condemned by God in any capacity. God graciously and justly gives all those who are in Christ eternal life through Him.

How do we understand the 'alls' in Romans 5 in light of federal headship? The first 'all' refers to all humans represented by Adam. In this case it is every single human being except for Jesus, who was born of a virgin. He is the sole exception to the fallen nature and death that awaits 'all' who are represented by Adam. That is why Romans 5:19

states: 'Through the one man's disobedience the many were made sinners.' The 'many' here refers to the 'all' who are represented in Adam.

But 'all' who are represented by Jesus through His federal headship will not die eternally, since Jesus has already paid that price for them, but will instead be declared fully justified through His saving work. Thus the 'all' in this instance refers not to every single human being who has ever lived, since that would mean universal salvation, but rather to 'all' who are united to Christ by faith. That is why Romans 5:19 is able to say: '... even so through the obedience of the One the *many* will be made righteous.' The 'all' represented in federal headship are 'many', but they are not the same 'all' that refers to every single human being who has ever lived.

This federal headship can be seen in God's gracious promise to Abraham in Genesis 12:1-4. There God promises to bless Abraham and the whole world through Abraham. But the passage does not mean that every single person in the entire world will be so blessed. Rather it means that people from every tongue, every tribe, and every nation will be blessed through Abraham. In other words, God did not intend to save every person through Abraham. But those whom He saves through Jesus are the fulfillment of the promise He gave to Abraham. We can see this in Revelation 7:9-10: 'After these things I looked, and behold, a great multitude which no one could count, from every nation and all tribes and people and tongues, standing before the throne and before the Lamb, clothed in white robes, and palm branches were in their hands; and they cry out with a loud voice, saying, "Salvation to our God who sits on the throne and to the Lamb"'. This is the group who is the 'all' whom Jesus represents in federal headship. It is also the 'many' but not 'all' of the people of the world. Thus, while there are universal aspects to God's salvation, meaning that He saves people from all over the world and not merely from one nation, we cannot say that Jesus' work of salvation is applied to every single person in the world.

Conclusion: Is Universalism biblical?

While there clearly are universal aspects of God's salvation through Jesus Christ, we cannot find universal salvation in the Bible. All of the disputed passages, read in their proper contexts and in the greater context of the storyline of the Bible, cannot and do not yield the results for which universalists hope. Furthermore, the doctrine of God and the love of God required by universalists is not the same love we see in the pages of the Bible. God's love cannot be redefined or reconstructed to fit any theory. He is who He is and does what He does. For these reasons we should, with respect, reject universalism as a viable biblical option.

What we do and believe in this life matters. There is no magic scenario in the Bible whereby all people everywhere are saved. If universalism were true, it would trivialize what we do in this life. Furthermore, it would also violate the consciences of those who are diametrically opposed to Jesus Christ. We will not all be saved from God's wrath in hell. Instead of upsetting us, this should make us more inclined than ever to cry out to Jesus for salvation. We must place our trust and faith in Him instead of desiring a universal salvation. To anyone who gives his or her life to Jesus, hell will not be an option on the day of judgment.

8

Conclusion

Throughout this book we have seen that God will carry out universal judgment on all humanity. He will do so in a way consistent with His love, holiness, righteousness, and justice.

- In chapter 1 we saw that God is the only being perfect enough to carry out this punishment.
- In chapter 2 we saw that God's attributes, including His love, work in concert with one another and never in isolation from each other. Thus the loving and holy God will pour out wrath on all who are not justified through Jesus Christ.
- In chapter 3 we saw that Jesus is the Son of God who speaks about hell as the authority on the subject because He is the Creator, sustainer, and One who will carry out divine wrath in hell.

- In chapter 4 we saw that the loving apostles continue the precise line of thinking on hell they received from their Master, Jesus.
- In chapter 5 we saw God's amazing love on display as He has created the only means of escape from hell by sending His Son to accomplish perfect salvation for the people of God.
- In chapter 6 we saw that hell is eternal and not any form of annihilation.
- In chapter 7 we saw that hell is eternal and will never be emptied.

In this final chapter, I want to conclude with a rough sketch of Revelation 20:10–21:8, as it is a vision that summarizes well much of the material in this book. Here we will see the Judge, the judged, and the judgment.[1]

THE JUDGE

Revelation 20:11 shows us God as the Judge. He is seen on His throne, as He is the sovereign King over creation. He alone is omniscient and therefore knows all things about all people. Every single thought or action is known by this God who has 'the books' opened before Him (Rev. 20:12). He

---

1   The terms and groups in this last section are from Christopher W. Morgan, *Christian Theology: The Biblical Story and Our Faith* (Nashville: B&H Academic, forthcoming).

will judge all people 'according to their deeds'. No one can thwart this Judge, as He is the supreme Lord.

THE JUDGED

There are no creatures immune to God's final judgment. Much like the beast and the false prophet, Satan himself will face the Lord and be judged for his deceiving actions (Rev. 20:10). Far from being a match for God, the Devil is merely one of those judged by this sovereign King. God will hold him accountable for every deed he has committed throughout his existence.

As the Judge summons forth all people, the creation gives up all of them. Both the living and the dead must stand before God: 'And the sea gave up the dead which were in it, and death and Hades gave up the dead which were in them; and they were judged, every one of them according to their deeds' (Rev. 20:13). All people everywhere will be summoned to give an account for their actions. No one can hide from God. No one can change his own fate at this moment. The books have been written and the judgment set.

THE JUDGMENT

God has declared that Satan, the beast, and the false prophet are guilty (Rev. 20:10). The Judge has sentenced them to an eternity in hell, the 'lake of fire and brimstone where ... they will be tormented day and night forever and ever'

(v. 10). There will never be a moment when they are not being punished for their crimes.

God has declared that there are two groups of people in this judgment. The first group are those people whose names are written in the book of life. This book contains the names of all of the people throughout human history who have placed their faith in Jesus Christ, the 'spring of the water of life' (Rev. 21:7). He has paid the price of God's just judgment for those who have faith in Him. He has forgiven their sins and made them righteous so that they cannot be condemned. Moreover, they are adopted into God's family, and He calls them 'sons' (v. 7).

The first group are those who are united to Christ by faith. They will be given the kingdom of God in heaven, or the new Jerusalem (Rev. 21:2). God will dwell with them and will 'wipe away every tear from their eyes; and there will no longer be any death; there will no longer be any mourning, or crying, or pain; the first things have passed away' (v. 4). All of life's pains and sorrows will be gone, and this group will be in the amazing presence of their Creator God for eternity. This is heaven, and it will never end.

But there is a second group.

The second group are those whose names are not written in the book of life (Rev. 20:15). Their deeds and sins are opened before the Judge, and He condemns them for their crimes. Some of their crimes are written for us to see. They are committed by 'the cowardly and unbelieving and abominable and murderers and immoral persons and sorcerers and idolaters and all liars' (v. 8). Since these people are not in Christ, His substitutionary death cannot be applied to them. Thus, they stand in their own guilt and will therefore pay the just penalty for their sins.

They will be cast into the lake of fire, where death, Hades, Satan, the beast, and the false prophet have already been cast (Rev. 20:8-14). This is the lake that burns with 'fire and brimstone, which is the second death' (21:8). There they too, just like Satan, will be 'tormented day and night forever and ever' (20:8). This is hell, and it will never end.

My hope is that you are convinced that hell is real and is the place into which all people without faith in Jesus Christ will be cast. It will be eternal in its punishment and destruction. It will also be a complete separation and banishment from any of God's kingdom blessings or common grace, leaving only His divine wrath. In light of these truths, there is one—and only one—hope for escape. Jesus Christ is our only hope. Turn your life over to Him. Bow your knees and confess that Jesus Christ is Lord, and He will be faithful to receive you.

Appendix

Frequently Asked Questions

In this section, I hope to answer a few of the questions most often asked concerning God and hell. All of these questions have already been addressed in various sections of the book, which contain fuller explanations (along with footnotes). However, here I want to give quick biblical responses to the most pressing questions concerning hell.

1. IS HELL REAL?

Yes, the Bible describes hell as a real place where the wicked will be punished for their sins by God for eternity. The Old Testament alludes to hell, Jesus both created and described it, and the apostles continued the teaching they received from Jesus. Both heaven and hell are part of the new creation and will exist throughout eternity (Rev. 21:1-8).

2. Does Satan rule hell?

Satan is not the ruler of hell. God is the Creator and ruler of all areas of the entire created order (including hell). Hell is a real place created by God as the place where He will dispense final and righteous judgment against the wicked. In Revelation 20:10 we read that Satan (also known as the Devil) will spend eternity in hell as he receives God's divine wrath: 'And the devil who deceived them was thrown into the lake of fire and brimstone, where the beast and the false prophet are also: and they will be tormented day and night forever and ever.' In other words, God is the ruler over hell. Satan will be in hell for eternity, but not as its sovereign ruler. Rather, he will be a recipient of God's just wrath.

3. Are the images of hell found in the Bible literal or figurative?

This is a complex question that requires a few responses in order to provide a complete answer. First, all of Scripture's images of hell are describing the realities of hell. So hell is all of the following at the same time: fire ('eternal fire', 'fiery furnace', 'unquenchable fire', 'everlasting fire', 'the lake of fire that burns with sulfur', and the place where 'the smoke of their torment goes up forever and ever'), darkness ('outer darkness' and 'banishment from God's covenant blessings'), punishment ('judgment', 'torment', 'eternal punishment', and 'weeping and gnashing of teeth'), and destruction ('death', 'second death', 'total ruin', and 'total loss').

Second, each of these images speaks truth. Since hell is the place where God pours out judgment against the wicked, hell is fire. The fire (judgment) of God in hell is eternal and therefore can be called eternal or everlasting fire. Is the fire of hell literal? It certainly could be. There are plenty of passages that describe hell as fire or as the lake of fire.

However, hellfire might also be an image that represents the all-consuming presence of God as He dispenses judgment against the wicked. In Exodus 19:18 God descended on Mount Sinai 'in fire; and its smoke ascended like the smoke of a furnace, and the whole mountain quaked violently' as God's glory appeared to the nation of Israel as a 'consuming fire' (Exod. 24:17). In Deuteronomy 4:24 Moses is warning the nation of Israel against idolatry. He describes God as a God who will carry out judgment against sin because 'the Lord your God is a consuming fire, a jealous God.'

Moses also describes God as a God who will destroy enemies as a 'consuming fire' (Deut. 9:3). Isaiah the prophet delivers a strong warning against the enemies of the people of God in Jerusalem. He warns: 'The multitude of your enemies will become like fine dust, and the multitude of the ruthless ones like the chaff which blows away; and it will happen instantly, suddenly. From the LORD of hosts you will be punished with thunder and earthquake and loud noise, with whirlwind and tempest and the flame of a consuming fire' (Isa. 29:5-6). Isaiah 29:27-30 also shows God's wrath to be displayed as a consuming fire, and the enemies of God will ask, 'Who among us can live with the consuming fire? Who among us can live with continual burning?' (33:14). Moreover, the book of Hebrews offers a strong warning for those who might consider turning away from Christ, since God would most certainly judge such action harshly: 'See to it that you do not refuse Him who is speaking. For if those did not escape when they refused him who warned them on earth, much less will we escape who turn away from Him who warns from heaven … for our God is a consuming fire' (Heb. 12:25-29).

Hell's fire might be a literal fire that engulfs the wicked in hell. Then again, fire might be an image that speaks to God's perfect wrath being poured out on His enemies. Fire might also be an image that speaks to hell's punishment. At the end of the day, whether literal or an image of a truthful reality, hell's fire is something one should seek to avoid.

Hell can also be described as 'outer darkness'. Jesus refers to hell as the place where His enemies will be thrown into 'outer darkness; in that place there will be weeping and gnashing of teeth' (Matt. 8:12; 22:13; 25:30). Does this mean that hell is a place of literal darkness? It could be a dark place, but it seems odd for hell to be both dark and an all-consuming fire at the same time (if we take both images literally). Rather, I think it is safest to say that 'outer darkness' speaks to the reality of covenant wrath. Just as hell can be described as separation from God's covenant blessings but not from His omnipresence, so too can we speak of hell as outer darkness.

I believe this imagery comes from the Old Testament book of Isaiah: 'The people who walk in darkness will see a great light; those who live in a dark land, the light will shine on them' (9:2). This passage is not speaking to nations that reside in places that are literally dark and lack light from the sun. Rather, this is imagery using 'light' in reference to those who are inside God's covenant and therefore able to receive God's covenant blessings, and 'darkness' in reference to those who are not in God's covenant and therefore only able to receive God's covenant curses or wrath. Thus I think that 'outer darkness' is an image that speaks to the true reality that those in hell will endure God's covenant wrath for eternity. Similarly, it might be stated that those in heaven are in 'eternal light' as they enjoy God's covenant blessings for eternity, as Revelation 21:22-27 suggests:

> I saw no temple in it, for the Lord God the Almighty and the Lamb are its temple. And the city has no need of the sun or of the moon to shine on it, for the glory of God has illumined it, and its lamp is the Lamb. The nations will walk by its light, and the kings of the earth will bring their glory into it. In the daytime

> (for there will be no night there) its gates will never be
> closed; and they will bring the glory and the honor of
> the nations into it; and nothing unclean, and no one
> who practices abomination and lying, shall ever come
> into it, but only those whose names are written in the
> Lamb's book of life.

It is in this same light that we should understand hell as 'banishment' from God's presence. Since God is omnipresent, He is, by definition, in all places at all times. This means that God was in hell at creation, is there presently, and will be there for eternity (as much as He was, is, and will be in heaven). However, hell is rightly understood as banishment from the presence of God. We should probably understand this to mean that those in hell will be banished from God's covenant blessing presence and will only receive God's eternal wrath. In other words, we should see this image in close proximity to hell as 'outer darkness', meaning that those there are outside of God's blessings and therefore capable only of receiving punishment.

As we have seen from these examples, I think that the images used to describe hell to us are just that—images. They are truthful and speak to us in pictures that describe hell's reality. Each of the images should be traced back to previous portions of the Bible in order to capture the biblical view of hell, rather than allowing our own imaginations to define these images. Furthermore, from my perspective, we can avoid some of the false teaching on hell if we allow all of the images of hell to speak to a comprehensive reality rather than wrongly focusing and forcing literalism on one or two images (as annihilationism does, for example).

4. WHY IS HELL ETERNAL WHEN IT SEEMS THAT HUMAN SINS ARE FINITE AND LIMITED?

At first glance, it appears that human sins are limited and finite. After all, it would seem that our sinning against God would cease at the conclusion of our earthly lives. If this were true, then one might think that God would be unjust if He carried out eternal punishment for a finite number of sins committed against Him.

In response, first, we know that God is just and is not anything other than perfectly righteous in all cases. This fact is true of God's punishment in hell as well. Thus, His dispensing of punishment in hell will always be in the right allotment and will never be unjust.

Second, we must also consider God's perfect nature as the One against whom all sins are committed. When an individual commits an assault against his or her neighbor, a certain punishment is deserved. However, when that same assault is carried out against the leader of a nation, the punishment is greater because the victim of the assault is greater in stature. Thus, as we think about a lifetime of sins committed against a perfect God, we should presume that the punishment for those crimes is far greater than we might think. In this case, the Bible states that the punishment for a lifetime of sins against an infinitely holy and righteous God is eternal punishment. This might be the correct answer even though some readers will not be satisfied by that response.

But I think there is more to this argument. The Bible describes the reaction of those in hell as gnashing their teeth (Matt. 8:12; 13:42; 13:50; 22:13; 24:51; 25:30; Luke 13:28). Certainly, one can think of gnashing of teeth as something one does when in pain. If we run our heads into an unseen beam, we might grit and grind our teeth together as we endure the pain. This image can certainly be true of those enduring God's divine wrath in hell. They might be gnashing their teeth in response to the pain of hell.

However, the Bible helps us to understand 'gnashing of teeth' in another capacity. Psalm 37:12 says: 'The wicked plots against the righteous and gnashes at him with his teeth.' It seems that the wicked person is not merely in pain but is seething in hatred toward the righteous. This idea is seen again in Psalm 35:15-16: 'At my stumbling they rejoiced and gathered themselves together; the smiters whom I did not know gathered together against me. They slandered me without ceasing. Like godless jesters at a feast, they gnashed at me with their teeth.' Again, this same idea is seen in Psalm 112:10, as the wicked gnash their teeth when they see how God blesses the righteous man. In all of these passages, it seems that gnashing one's teeth is a sign that one is against and contrary to another. In Acts 7:2-53 Stephen speaks against the sins of the Jewish leaders. In 7:54 they respond in anger and hatred as they 'were cut to the quick, and they began gnashing their teeth at him.' This is the meaning behind the gnashing of teeth in hell. Those who are in hell are contrary and opposed to God in their hearts and therefore respond outwardly in defiance against Him by gnashing their teeth. In other words, those who gnash their teeth at God are sinning against Him.

Furthermore, we must also remember that God grants eternality to all people at the final resurrection. Thus He gives eternal life to those who will be in heaven and eternal death to those who will be in hell. Those in heaven will respond with right worship and praise as they enjoy their eternal life. Those in hell will respond to God by 'gnashing their teeth' at Him as they endure their punishment. As they gnash their teeth at God, they continue to sin against God throughout eternity. In this way, the wicked will endure eternal punishment by God because of their lifetime of sins committed against Him as well as those they continue to commit against Him in hell. Seen in this manner, one's sins are never finite but continue throughout eternity in hell. Thus God's punishment is right and just and never excessive.

5. IF HELL IS SO AWFUL, AND GOD WANTS TO SAVE PEOPLE, THEN WHY DOES GOD NOT ALLOW PEOPLE TO REPENT IN HELL?

At first glance, this appears to be a legitimate question. But it makes a major assumption that we should not grant. It assumes that there will be people in hell who will want to repent from their sins and turn to saving faith in Jesus Christ. In order to answer this question, therefore, we must understand two primary truths: we must come to grips with what the Bible says about our sin nature and what it says about opportunities to repent after death.

First, the Bible says that every human being inherits a fallen sin nature (Rom. 5). This sin nature means that each of us is 'dead in [our] trespasses and sins' (Eph. 2:1). This fallen sin nature desires human autonomy and freedom to live after the lusts of the flesh and is contrary to God (Eph. 2:2-3). In this fallen nature, we do not and cannot please God, since we are hostile toward Him and His law (Rom. 8:7-8). Left in this condition, we will never desire to love God rightly and therefore will be left to face His wrath (Eph. 2:3). Unfortunately, every person in hell is still in this fallen sin nature and therefore will not desire to repent and come to saving faith in Jesus Christ (the only means by which anyone can enter heaven). While those in hell might desire to end their punishment, they will never want it badly enough to follow God's plan of salvation even if they were able to do so.

Second, the Bible gives no hope that anyone will be offered a chance at salvation after death. Hebrews 9:27 seems to show that the opposite is true as it says: 'it is appointed for men to die once and after this comes judgment.' In other words, God gives us our current life in order to repent from our sin and turn toward Jesus Christ in faith. The decisions and choices we make in this life are what determine our ultimate destiny. Once we die, our eternal destinations are set and cannot be revoked (Luke 16:26). Furthermore, when we combine this truth with our previous point, we also understand that those in hell will not desire Jesus Christ enough to repent. In other words, even if God did allow the opportunity (which He does not) for those in hell to repent from their sins and come to Jesus Christ in saving faith, they would not. It would be contrary to their nature, will, and desire. Thus God is completely just in not allowing a post-mortem opportunity for salvation.

6. **If hell is so awful, and God does not want people to end up there, then why does He not provide more warning about it?**

Before we answer this question, we should acknowledge the assumptions behind it. First, it assumes that God is not doing enough to warn people about judgment. He has either failed to give warning to people or failed to give them enough warning. Second, it assumes that people (some or perhaps all) will recognize the warnings and respond in a way that allows them to escape God's judgment. Both of these assumptions are addressed below as we answer this question in four parts, addressing: 1) God's universal warnings found in creation; 2) God's universal warnings found in conscience; 3) God's warnings through His Word; and 4) humanity's response to God's warnings.

First, God has warned (and continues to warn) all people through creation. Psalm 19:1-4 says: 'The heavens are telling of the glory of God; and their expanse is declaring the work of His hands. Day to day pours forth speech, and night to night reveals knowledge. There is no speech, nor are there words; their voice is not heard. Their voice has gone out through all the earth, and their utterances to the end of the world.' The creation itself is God's canvas upon which He is revealing Himself. All of His creatures know, merely by observing the created order, that God is good, powerful, wise, and to be obeyed. Although it does not have a literal voice, creation speaks a universal language that reveals God. Creation's testimony does not cease in its proclamation of God. Each moment, day and night, the creation broadcasts who God is and that He is to be served rightly.

This same truth is found in Romans. Paul states that creation speaks volumes about God: '... because that which is known about God is evident within them; for God made it evident to them. For since the creation of the world His invisible attributes, His eternal power and divine nature, have been clearly seen, being understood through what has been made, so that they are without excuse' (Rom. 1:19-20). God has made enough of Himself evident in creation that every created thing without exception should know Him. And they do know God. They know that He is infinitely powerful, good, and to be obeyed. In other words, creation stands as a consistent and successful warning to all people everywhere that they must serve God rightly or else face His judgment.

Furthermore, creation does not cease in its warning of divine judgment: 'For the wrath of God is revealed from heaven against all ungodliness and unrighteousness of men who suppress the truth in unrighteousness' (Rom. 1:18). As long as creation stands, so too does God's universal warning of judgment against those who rebel against the Creator God. This warning is unceasing and universal.

Second, God has warned all people through conscience. Paul states that there is a universal law placed inside each human being so that all know right from wrong: 'For when Gentiles who do not have the Law do instinctively the things of the Law, these, not having the Law, are a law to themselves, in that they show the work of the Law written in their hearts, their conscience bearing witness and their thoughts alternately accusing or else defending them' (Rom. 2:14-15). All people are innately aware of who God is and that He requires obedience. When we break His laws, we know it intuitively. When we lie, we know it. When we steal, we know that our actions are wrong, as our conscience censures us. Furthermore, our conscience serves as a constant reminder that God will punish those who break His laws. The conscience is a worldwide and continuous warning in each human being throughout the duration of their lives that tells us that we will be held accountable for our thoughts and actions.

Through creation and conscience, God has revealed Himself to all people and warned them without pause. One could say that there has never been a moment of our lives when God was not warning us about divine judgment for rebelling against Him. In fact, one might better ask, what more could God do to warn us of His judgment?

This brings us to our third point: God has further warned people about judgment through His Word. Chapters 3–4 of this book include many statements whereby Jesus and His apostles have warned people of God's wrath against those who fail to obey Him. Jesus alerts His listeners, 'Every tree that does not bear good fruit is cut down and thrown into the fire' (Matt. 7:19), and, 'So it will be… that the angels will come forth and take out the wicked from the righteous, and will throw them into the furnace of fire; in that place there will be weeping and gnashing of teeth' (Matt. 13:49-50). In fact, every single New Testament author offers some sort of teaching or warning on hell. The message of hell is one spoken not out of hatred but out of love.

God has warned all people everywhere about divine wrath through creation and conscience. No one can truthfully claim that God has failed to give sufficient warning (Rom. 1:20). His warnings are more specific in His Word. There He shows hell's nature and eternal duration. Because of these threefold warnings, no one can plead ignorance on the day of judgment. Moreover, no one can say that he or she did not receive enough warning.

Since all people have obtained (and are currently obtaining) constant warnings about God's judgment for law-breaking, we must understand what humanity does with such warnings. This is our fourth point: we tend to quash God's warnings and live as though universal judgment will not occur. This final point can itself be made in four ways.

First, Paul reminds us that we are rebellious law-breakers who scoff at God and His laws. By nature we are unrighteous creatures who live for ourselves, in blatant disregard for God:

> The wrath of God is revealed from heaven against all ungodliness and unrighteousness of men, who by their unrighteousness suppress the truth. For what can be known about God is plain to them, because God has shown it to them. For his invisible attributes, namely

> his eternal power and divine nature have been clearly perceived, ever since the creation of the world, in the things that have been made. So they are without excuse. For although they knew God, they did not honor him as God or give thanks to him, but they became futile in their thinking, and their foolish hearts were darkened. Claiming to be wise, they became fools, and exchanged the glory of the immortal God for images resembling mortal man and birds and animals and creeping things. (Rom 1:18-23, ESV)

Since our hearts are dark and directed inward, we suppress God's truth. This truth is everything that we know about God through creation and conscience. This means we suppress the truth about God's nature, power, and warnings about judgment.

Second, we not only suppress God's truth but also exchange it for a falsehood. Instead of perceiving God's truth and acting accordingly, we rebel against our Creator and attempt to place other created things in God's place (Rom. 1:23). It is ironic that we tend to exchange God for created things that cannot ultimately judge us as we know God will. Thus, as we live in this false exchange, the Bible rightly says that we are fools as we know one set of truths but live in contradiction to it (Rom. 1:22). In this irrational state, we not only live as though God does not exist but also give hearty approval to others who do the same (Rom. 1:32).

For our purposes, the constant and unceasing warning of judgment that God gives us is perceived and known to all people but is ignored and explained away as something cruel and unwarranted.

Third, as we judge other's actions, we display that we know there is one God who will judge our actions. All of us have called another to account for wrongdoing. We have all seen someone commit an act that we think is unjust, and we have all said something like 'Do not lie to me' or 'You are being hateful.' The Bible claims this action not only is hypocritical but also shows that we know there is a universal standard holding us accountable for misconduct:

> You have no excuse, O man, every one of you who judges. For in passing judgment on another you condemn yourself, because you, the judge, practice the very same things. We know that the judgment of God rightly falls on those who practice such things. Do you suppose O man—you who judge those who practice such things and yet do them yourself—that you will escape the judgment of God? (Rom. 2:1-3, ESV)

In other words, our act of judging actions proves that we know there is a God who will call all evil into judgment. Furthermore, since we are guilty of the same violations that we accuse others of, we know we will be rightly judged by God.

Finally, since we are aware of the judgment looming over us, we have a decision to make. Either we can continue to live in foolishness as we presume upon God's grace or we can repent of our law-breaking and turn to faith in Jesus Christ (see chapter 5). For those who shrug off God's warnings, the Bible warns: 'Because of your hard and impenitent heart you are storing up wrath for yourself on the day of wrath when God's righteous judgment will be revealed ... for those who are self-seeking and do not obey the truth, but obey unrighteousness, there will be wrath and fury' (Rom. 2:5-8, ESV). However, for those who recognize that they have violated God's laws, repent, and trust in Jesus, the Bible says that God will give them eternal life (v. 7).

7. HOW CAN THE SAVED BE ETERNALLY HAPPY KNOWING THAT SOME OF THEIR LOVED ONES ARE IN HELL?

Before we answer, please allow me to state that I am not a 'hell-monger' who wants to see people go to hell. Part of my agreeing to write this book was due to my hope that those who read it will turn to Jesus Christ in faith and escape God's judgment. Furthermore, I am a pastor and have committed my life to telling people about Jesus so that they will not go to hell.

We will answer this question in four parts. First, we will remind ourselves of our fallen nature that hinders our current perspective. Second, we will see that those who are saved will not possess a fallen nature in heaven and therefore will have a view of hell that sees God's actions as just and even praiseworthy. Third, the Bible does not show those who are saved as bearing any encumbrance to their joy in heaven. Fourth, while God gives us life today, we should be burdened for those who do not know Jesus as the only means to escape hell. Let's consider each of these four points in more detail.

First, we must remind ourselves that we are fallen people, with fallen emotions and senses. Our sense of justice ebbs and flows with culture and changes over times and seasons in our lives. What we think is right today might change tomorrow. This fluctuation shows us that our senses are slightly off and therefore are inconsistent. In other words, we see things differently than God does.

As we look at sin through our fallen perspectives, we do not see sin rightly. We tend to think that sin is 'not that big of a deal'. We do not think that sin against God should be punished by an eternity in hell because, well, 'everyone sins' and 'nobody is perfect'. Since this is our prevailing understanding of sin, we also tend to think of hell as unjust. Furthermore, when we think about someone we love in hell, it makes us angry and sad. But our anger tends to be directed at God instead of at sin. We highlight our fallen nature and inability to see things correctly when we recognize that our current nature will undergo a change.

The Bible says that those who are saved will receive a glorified nature. Romans 8:16-17 assures: 'The Spirit Himself testifies with our spirit that we are the children of God, and if children, heirs also, heirs of God and fellow heirs with Christ, if indeed we suffer with Him so that we may also be glorified with Him.' Again, Paul states: 'And not only this, but also we ourselves, having the first fruits of the Spirit, even we ourselves groan within ourselves, waiting eagerly for our adoption as sons, the redemption of our body' (v. 23). Everyone who believes in Jesus Christ for salvation will receive a glorified nature in heaven.

Along with that changed nature will come a change in perspective. The Bible promises: 'Beloved, now we are children of God, and it has not appeared as yet what we will be. We know that when He appears, we will be like Him, because we will see Him just as He is' (1 John 3:2). John is saying that we will understand things rightly since we will see God rightly. Because we will understand God rightly, we will also perceive sin for what it is, namely, total rebellion against a perfect God, requiring judgment.

In Revelation 19:1-2 the voices of the redeemed can be heard in their glorified nature as they sing praise to God for His work of just judgment: 'Hallelujah! Salvation and glory and power belong to our God. Because His judgments are true and righteous; for He has judged the great harlot who was corrupting the earth with her immorality, and He has avenged the blood of His bond servants on her.' This collection of believers is not a bloodthirsty group that longs to see people punished out of spite or vindictiveness. Rather, these people are praising God from their glorified nature and understand that God must punish evil. Since they understand sin rightly and comprehend God rightly, they are able to praise God for carrying out universal justice.

Charles Spurgeon (a British Baptist preacher; 1834–1892) illustrated this same point as he told a story about a mother and her children on the day of judgment:

> You must seek God for yourself, or rather God must seek you. You must have a vital experience of godliness in your heart, or else you are lost, even though all of your friends were in heaven. That was a dreadful dream which a pious mother once had, and told to her children. She thought the judgment day was come. The great books were opened. They all stood before God. And Jesus Christ said, 'Separate the chaff from the wheat; put the goats on the left hand, and the sheep on the right.' The mother dreamed that she and her children were standing just in the middle of the great assembly. And the angel came, and said, 'I must take the mother: she is a sheep: she must go to the right hand. The children are goats: they must go to the left.' She thought as she went her children clutched her, and said, 'Mother, can we part? Must we be separated?' She then put her arms around them, and seemed to say, 'My children, I would, if possible, take you with me.' But in a moment the angel touched her: her cheeks were

> dried, and, now, overcoming natural affection, being
> rendered supernatural and sublime, resigned to God's
> will, she said, 'My children, I taught you well, I trained
> you up, and you forsook the ways of God, and now all
> I have to say is, Amen to your condemnation.'

This illustration highlights the fact that our perspectives will change as we understand things rightly for the first time. When we are in heaven, the knowledge of a loved one in hell will not make us sad or angry. Rather, we will agree that God has done the right and just thing in judging all those who break His laws apart from forgiveness in Christ. It does not mean that we will love those people less, but it does mean that we will love God far more.

When I was in fourth grade, I broke a known school rule. The violation was serious enough that I was called to the principal's office. There, she told me that she was sending a note home with me seeking permission from my parents to swat me. I remember thinking that my dad, who loved me very much, might deny the request thus allowing me to avoid being swatted with a wooden paddle by the principal. In this assumption, I was wrong.

Upon reading the principal's note, my father did three things. First, he asked me if I had broken the school rule. I admitted my guilt to him thinking that my admission would lessen the severity of my punishment. Second, upon my confession of guilt, he then told me that he loved me and gave a good swat. Third, he wrote a note to the principal which I had to take back to her. It said, 'Yes, you do have permission to swat Ben. Also, you do not need my permission again. If he violates a school rule that you deem worthy of a swat, then you have my advanced permission to carry out that punishment.'

My dad is not (nor was he) a hard man. He is one of the few people on this earth who loves me unconditionally. When he agreed to my being punished, it was out of love. If I was guilty, then I should be punished in a just manner.

I believe this is how we will see heaven and hell. We will love God and understand that sin is cosmic treason against Him. We will also love our loved ones. But if God judges them guilty and sentences them to hell, then we will agree that God has made the right decision.

Third, the Bible shows that all believers are filled with joy in heaven. In Revelation 20–21 the Bible shows both heaven and hell as part of the new creation. Furthermore, there is no hint that believers are lacking joy in any capacity. In fact, their tears will be wiped away as there will be 'no longer any death; there will no longer be any mourning, or crying, or pain; the first things have passed away' (Rev. 21:4). Sadness and regret are emotions that belong to this world. But in heaven we will be changed and will not lack any joy nor have any moment of sadness. Our joy will be complete as we find it in God. In other words, the knowledge of loved ones in hell will not take away any joy that believers will have in heaven.

Fourth, while we are still here in this life, we must be burdened for those who are currently headed for hell. So long as God gives us breath and occasion, we should be broken over those who do not know Jesus Christ. We must spend our remaining days praying for the lost and seeking opportunities to proclaim the loving hope of Jesus Christ to them. In other words, we should not spend our days angry at God for what He will do in hell. Rather, we must be thankful that God has provided an escape from hell and warn others about hell in the hope that they too will repent and turn to Jesus in saving faith.

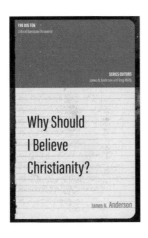

Why Should I Believe Christianity?

JAMES N. ANDERSON

Some people boldly claim, 'Christianity is fine for some, but it isn't for me'. Others feel it is just outdated and irrelevant. For better or worse, everyone in the Western world has come into contact with Christianity: we all have some opinion on it.

James N. Anderson, with a clear, humorous logic, explores what Christianity really claims, and shows the underlying reason and consistency behind these claims. By the end of *Why Should I Believe Christianity?*, while you may not agree with the Christian worldview, it is impossible to be left sitting on the fence.

ISBN 978-1-7819-1869-2

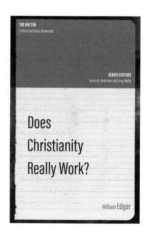

Does Christianity Really Work?

William Edgar

Wasn't the South African Apartheid supported by Christians? Weren't the Crusades motivated by greed, but advocated by the church? Don't phoney television preachers manipulate viewers into donating money? William Edgar addresses these and other questions honestly, without attempting to dismiss or explain away their uncomfortable realities. He displays the good aspects of the church even more brilliantly through frankly and Biblically acknowledging the bad. If you have ever asked the question *Does Christianity Really Work?* this will be an interesting and enlightening read, whatever your prior convictions.

ISBN 978-1-7819-1775-6

Why Is There Evil in the World (and So Much of It?)

GREG WELTY

Many people argue that the presence of evil in the world is proof that God cannot exist, or if He does exist, cannot be good or all-powerful.

Greg Welty uses biblical exegesis alongside his experience as a philosopher to present a different conclusion. God, the sovereign Creator and Sustainer of the world, really does work all things for good. A must-read for anyone struggling with this issue.

ISBN 978-1-5271-0141-8

Christian Focus Publications

Our mission statement –

STAYING FAITHFUL

In dependence upon God we seek to impact the world through literature faithful to His infallible Word, the Bible. Our aim is to ensure that the Lord Jesus Christ is presented as the only hope to obtain forgiveness of sin, live a useful life and look forward to heaven with Him.

Our books are published in four imprints:

CHRISTIAN
FOCUS

Popular works including biographies, commentaries, basic doctrine and Christian living.

CHRISTIAN
HERITAGE

Books representing some of the best material from the rich heritage of the church.

MENTOR

Books written at a level suitable for Bible College and seminary students, pastors, and other serious readers. The imprint includes commentaries, doctrinal studies, examination of current issues and church history.

CF4•K

Children's books for quality Bible teaching and for all age groups: Sunday school curriculum, puzzle and activity books; personal and family devotional titles, biographies and inspirational stories – because you are never too young to know Jesus!

Christian Focus Publications Ltd,
Geanies House, Fearn, Ross-shire,
IV20 1TW, Scotland, United Kingdom.
www.christianfocus.com